Chinese Tasty Tales Cookbook

by GARY LEE

Published by   Chinese Treasure Productions
                P.O. Box 15114
                San Francisco
                California 94115
Simultaneously in the U.S.A. and the United Kingdom
Copyright protected under terms of the Berne Convention
All Rights Reserved except for use in a review

Distributed by ◖ J. Philip O'Hara, Inc.
                   20 East Huron
                   Chicago 60611

LC: 74-9181
ISBN: 0-87955-314-6
Printed and bound in Hong Kong
First Printing 1974

Table of Contents

津津集

李一印著　張大千題

ABOUT THE COVER

My late father was a serious collector of Chinese brush painting. During my boyhood, I was accustomed to help him to put his collection on the walls, changed them according to the seasons and moods, as my father had too many masterpieces through life long seeking famous painters' artworks.

For Chinese who appreciate fine art, a painting is not used for decorating the walls, but to immerse themselves in admiring the painter's talents which give enjoyment endlessly. Among hundreds of famous painters, Professor Chang Dai-chien was the one I had known when I was young boy, and also the only Chinese I know who is a poet, calligrapher and a painter of all fields. Most painters limit themself to only one field, such as birds, quadrupeds, flowers, cloud and waterfalls, landscapes, bamboos and rocks, portraits, easy-going-style, or finely in details. Professor Chang excels in all of them!

I have known Professor Chang in person during my stay in Brasil of many years but I never had the courage to mention about my father's name, this is very Chinese, because I felt I was not achieving what my late father expected me to be! So, if I could not honor my father, I would prefer not to let others know that I am the son of so and so!

Miserably I need a cover for this book in a given time for very unpleasant and complicated reason. I prefer to take either Eighty or Eight! So I decided to let the cover be without anything but English lettering, or why don't I try to ask Professor Chang? Surprisingly he gave me a hand just like that!

I am sure that my late father would be very proud of me for having this cover done by Professor Chang. For my part, I really don't know how much I am honored by Professor Chang, who is now 74 with eye-sight suffering years after several operations, yet he finished the cover for this book.

My prose is poor but my sincere gratitude is genuine.

Professor Chang Dai-chien, Pebble Beach, 1974.

DEDICATIONS

Many of my friends built their homes in their spare time with good workmanship, but none of them dare to claim that they completed it without others hands.

I, therefore, feel it is natural to mention these warm hands with love, or how could I write?

To friends who attend my cooking class: whose enthusiasm turns my job into enjoyment, I joyfully write.

To my family members scattered around the world: for longing of whom, I yearningly write.

To my late parents and teachers who expected me to learn and be diligent, do my best and keep away from evil: in remembering them, I conscientiously write.

To friends who never tired of helping me with my messy drafts, I carefreely write.

To the magnificent sunset: which constantly reminds me that the night is near, so I must write, write, write!

INTRODUCTION

If you like to cook and also read Chinese tales, then this book is especially written for you. All of the tales are based on traditional folklore. A few additional touches have been included to make them more readable. I avoided the use of the original Chinese names as much as possible because of the difficulty in pronunciation. The recipes have been fully tested and are presented in such detail that you will be able to follow them easily.

I was born into an old-fashioned Chinese family and given a classical Chinese education which, of course, included a study of our history. I have been a restaurateur, a chef, and am presently teaching Chinese cooking in the San Francisco Bay area. Fortunately, my varied background has greatly aided me in my writings. I don't know how I came upon the idea of linking tales with recipes. It has proven to be quite a task!

I limited myself to tales of general interest only and, in so doing, tried to retain the character of Chinese subtleness. The recipes are varied not only in ingredients, but also in cooking methods. Although the number is small, they cover a wide range of Chinese cooking, and I sincerely invite you to venture into this seemingly mysterious culinary jungle. If you will only walk through the first row of confusing brush and trees you will find, inside that jungle, a Shangri-la.

In writing this book, I have drawn heavily on my resources of knowledge and experience. However, it will have been well worth the endeavor if you, the reader, find something interesting and useful.

Many persons have made it possible for me to write these tales and recipes. In addition to members of my family, this number includes teachers, schoolmates, colleagues, strangers, and our housemaids and cooks, all of whom have a share in the merits of this book. My sad regret is that not all of them will ever read it. However, I remember all of "you" deeply in my heart.
Peace.

GARY LEE
HONG KONG
October 2, 1972

The Peach of Longevity

According to legend, The Mother lived in the Ninth Heaven. She had a peach tree in her garden which bore the peaches of longevity. The tree was planted in pebbles of jade and ruby, so the leaves were a shiny everlasting green and the fruit was blushing red. The tree took one hundred years to bloom, two hundred years to bear fruit, and another three hundred years to mature. Furthermore, it bore only three fruits at a time.

Now and again, The Mother gave one of the peaches to some deserving person on his birthday as a blessed gift. When such a gift was granted, the lucky recipient would live to be more than one hundred years old.

The peaches were everlasting and, even though their production was so low, after billions of years, The Mother had many peaches in her garden because she had found so few people deserving of them. Although no one in the Ninth Heaven needed the Peaches of Longevity, they were still guarded carefully for fear that someone might steal one, bring it to our world, and barter it at any price.

Since no one in our world could buy such a peach, the Chinese made a "peach" from dough to celebrate an aged person's birthday. For birthdays of young people, only noodles were served, as the lengthy noodles signify a long future.

Once there was a scholar who was very wise and witty—naughty, too. He was invited to a banquet and was ordered by the mayor of the town to compose a poem to celebrate the birthday of the mayor's mother. In front of the guests, the scholar swiftly wrote the following lines:

THIS WOMAN IS NOT A LADY, BECAUSE
HER SON ATTEMPTS TO BE A THIEF

When he had finished these lines, he paused and sipped his tea. The guests were all shocked because of his extreme rudeness in insulting the mayor of the town. The mayor was very angry indeed.

"How dare you, you little animal! Guards! Arrest him and charge him with insulting the mayor!"

"Wait, your Honor," said the scholar, with a confident smile. "I have not finished my verse."

He picked up the brush and completed the verse so that it had four lines, which was traditional for a Chinese poem. It now read:

> THIS WOMAN IS NOT A LADY
> Because she is an angel from heaven.
> HER SON ATTEMPTS TO BE A THIEF
> To steal a Peach of Longevity for his mother.

This tale has no ending. It is a play on words, as many Chinese know. Because steamed buns have already been associated with the story of the Barbarian's Head, and since the Peach of Longevity would only be a different shape formed from the same dough, the moral is that you are filling a different bottle with the same wine, so a noodle dish is chosen here.

The Chinese give birthday wishes as "Long live a hundred years." I would like to alter this wish to "Live long happily."

CHINESE NOODLES IN GENERAL:

There are too many varieties of noodles to list them all. Here are some representative selections of this Chinese-created food.

Number of Servings: Of the Chinese fresh noodles made with eggs, each pound will serve four full portions generously as a one-course meal. Used as a complementary dish, it will make up to 12 servings, such as in a buffet party, accompanied by four or five courses.

The First Cooking: It is very simple, but important for the result of this dish that you use sufficient water to cover the batch of noodles. DON'T ADD ANY SALT TO THE WATER! It will soften the noodles too much. A little oil will prevent the noodles sticking together during cooking.

Noodles should be cooked in an uncovered vessel, so that you can check doneness and avoid boiling over of the water. They should not be cooked too long, however, as fresh noodles only require 2 to 4 minutes (after returning to a boil). Strain and immediately rinse them thoroughly with cold tap water.

Here are two methods for using noodles:

For immediate use in soup form: Just drain and use them as soon as possible.
For Chinese-fried style: Place the colander in the sink and oil the still draining batch of noodles from the surface. The oil will go down while the excess water will always dissipate one second earlier. Wait for a few minutes, then use your hands to transfer the noodles into a roasting pan, then gently intermix the top and bottom portions for even oiling. They can be kept overnight, covered to prevent drying out of the top layer.

Broth to be used for Noodles in Soup Form: Chicken broth is the best choice. However, another light kind of broth may be substituted if it is not greasy. Heat the cooked noodles in broth, season to taste and serve with the following suggested variations. The meat part could be any stew. Vegetable part is your choice.
Here is an example:

Heat the cooked noodles in broth, add a few leaves of lettuce, which need only 30 seconds to soften, yet retain their crunchiness. Serve in individual bowls. Top with several slices or chunks of stewed beef.

One-Step Variation Without Using Broth: (for four servings)

  4 oz. pork strips, marinated in dark marinade
  2 cups Chinese Cabbage strips
  2 T. cooking oil

Start with hot oil, cook the pork strips and, after 30 seconds, add cabbage strips. Fill with about 4 cups of water, season with salt to taste, add soy sauce and a pinch of pepper. Cover and cook for ten minutes, add the pre-cooked noodles and bring to boiling. Wait for another 30 seconds, (boiling does not mean that the noodles are hot enough to serve) and then serve.

AN ELEGANT WAY TO SERVE NOODLES IN SOUP FORM.

At one hand, the noodles are warm enough in seasoned broth. Cook a batch of Chinese-fried dish, such as Three Blessing Star in strips form. Fill the bowl first with drained noodles, then top neatly with the cooked strips which have been thickened with a little cornstarch. Finally, use a ladle to fill the bowl with broth, carefully from the side to prevent disturbing the pleasing form of the cooked strips.

General Information About Noodles to be Chinese-fried:
You have two choices.
(1) Using a heated wok or skillet, add the oiled noodles, and some broth or water. Very little is required, because it will be used only to produce enough steam to heat the noodles. At the same time, you may add salt and soy sauce to taste, then blend some meat and vegetables with the heated batch.

(2) Use 1 T. oil, cook the oiled noodles at medium low heat. Leave them spread out flat. After approximately 5 minutes, turn the entire batch by flipping the skillet or wok or by using a spatula. Heat the other side also, until both sides are crispy brown. The degree of crispness varies according to personal taste. Put on a plate. Normally, it will stay together forming a round cake. At the same time, cook a dish—for example, Three Blessing Stars, but with more sauce. When the sauce is done, pour it evenly over the top of the crispy brown

noodles. It is not necessary to season the noodles, because the sauce gives this dish a delightful taste.

Some more information about noodles: For soup form, use noodles of medium thickness; for Chinese-fried, use rather thin ones; for hot-mixing type, use the wider variety; and here is another recipe:
Hot-mixing: Cook the noodles as usual, reheat with boiling water and drain. In the meantime,

Heat 1 T. oil per serving—very hot, until smoking
1 T. chopped green onions (per serving)
1 T. chopped ginger root
1 T. chopped fresh coriander

Arrange the drained noodles in a bowl, place all the chopped greens on top and burn them all with that hot oil. What a simple, yet effective, method of cooking! Season the entire batch with a little salt and some soy sauce to taste. Mix well and you will be amazed how such simple ingredients can produce such a delicious dish. If Chinese Oyster Sauce (in bottles ready for use) is available, add 1 t. per bowlful.

A WORD OR TWO ABOUT THE RECIPE DETAILS

Between Chinese, we never give each other recipes in much detail. We simply name the ingredients and the basic cooking method, such as deep-fry, steam, Chinese-fry, etc. We might mention that the taste should be sweet or sour; or perhaps suggest that the dish be seasoned with garlic and salt. However, since most of my readers may not have complete—or even basic—knowledge of Chinese cooking, I decided to include **every** detail so you could not fail to achieve the desired result.

I have learned to do many things from studying good books, and therefore have tried to be very thorough, down to the smallest detail. In such detail, the recipes may appear to be somewhat lengthy, but I do want you to be able to understand and to use each recipe with success.

I believe that to know twenty recipes thoroughly is much more worthwhile than to collect a thousand and not have the ability to use any one of them.

ON SERVING A DINNER AND BEING A HOST—AT THE SAME TIME

Since a Chinese dinner always consists of many courses, it is usually believed that either you must limit the quality and variety of courses—or you will not be able to join your guests. This is not true. This dilemma can be resolved with a different compromise.

Study your menu carefully. By planning ahead, you can have most of the dishes ready to serve. You have no problem with the soup; you can also offer dishes which are already done or going to be done without losing their quality. For instance, a deep-fried dish can be kept in the oven, heated to 180 degrees, with the door of the oven partially open. A steamed dish can be placed in the steamer, provided you can calculate correctly the time of serving. Then, as the Chinese dinner should include not only courses of different kinds of meat, but also various methods of preparation, all you actually have to do just before serving is cook one Chinese-fry dish. Sound tricky? No, it is only a matter of becoming accustomed to the way of cooking, and you can always include one cold dish which you have prepared even days ahead.

For westerners, to write a Chinese word is to draw a picture. For many Chinese, to remember only the 26 letters in the English alphabet is more than four dozens of live silk worms—to them even the capital letters M and N are the same silk worm!

The same principle applies to cooking—it is simple once you become accustomed to it. I recall that my grandfather had many faithful and efficient hands in his exporting business. One old respectful man managed to memorize all the 26 English letters used for marking the packages, but he could not pronounce the letter W. He **could** pronounce the letter M. So he referred to W as "the-reversed-M." If you have some difficulty in Chinese Cooking, please think about this old man and the way he managed to get his job done. Although not perfect, it was very passable—which was enough.

In the foregoing suggestions for preparing your menu, the Cold Dish was prepared ahead; soup is warmed; deep-frying dish is kept in the oven; you place the steamed dish in the steamer; cook the one Chinese-fry dish; and announce the dinner. When you have all the food on the table, the Steaming dish is about done. So—walk gracefully out of the kitchen and enjoy your Chinese dinner with your guests!

The Hidden Dagger

During the Warring States 481-221 B.C., there lived a king who was hated by many of his people for his cruelty. The king realized that he was constantly under the shadow of possible assassination by his subjects because of his despicable treatment of them. Therefore, he was very careful to protect himself, especially if he was invited to dine.

One very "thoughtful" banquet invitation was offered to the king and he confidently accepted. He was certain that, since he would not be the first one to taste the food, the chance of being poisoned would be very small. Of course, all the servants preparing and serving the banquet would be thoroughly searched by his body-guards to make sure that no fatal weapons were concealed.

The banquet for the king lasted for hours and everything went smoothly until the last main course —a fish—was being served. Fish, in Chinese custom, means the party is coming to its end, as the pronunciation of "Fish" is similar to the word of a goodwill saying which is "May goodness remain." Noth-  ing had happened up to now and the waiters were serving the last course as efficiently as the first course.

The assigned waiter who was serving the king was slight in build with a pale complexion. He always worked very slowly and calmly when serving. As this last dish was being brought to the side of the king, the waiter's face became even paler! It was a large whole fish with a lot of sauce—apparently delightful and delicious; but actually a thin-bladed dagger had been hidden in

the stomach of the fish when the cooks prepared it in the kitchen.

The small pale waiter suddenly abandoned his slow, calm manner. He swiftly dug his hand into the fish, grasped the dagger and with the speed of lightning, stabbed the king one time—and that was enough!

SWEET & SOUR FISH (Whole, with sauce—the Eastern Chinese style)

1 fish, about 2 lbs, of rock cod type with no tiny bones
1/4 cup of red vinegar
1/4 cup of sugar
1/4 cup of ketchup
1/4 cup of broth
1/10 cup of soy sauce
1/5 cup of cooking oil
some cornstarch to be used for thickening

Cook all the listed ingredients for sauce at medium heat for about 5 minutes. Proper simmering without covering will cut the sharp taste of vinegar.

Using a sharp knife, make several intersecting incisions on both sides of the fish—about 1/4 to 1/2 inch in depth. The cutting should be diagonal and at an angle, which improves the shape of the fish after deep-frying.

Sprinkle the fish all over with salt, dust it with flour, and deep-fry it at 350 degrees until brown. Here is a simple trick for serving the fish at its best quality: just deep-fry it hours ahead, re-deep-fry it when it is to be served. Although you perform one more operation in deep-frying, the crispier quality and less time required during the busy serving hour will be well worth your effort involved in the first frying. To serve, re-deep-fry the fish, while the sauce is bubbling. Place the fish on a platter and pour the hot sweet and sour sauce over the fish.

PREPARING THE MENU FOR A DINNER PARTY

Knowing hundreds of recipes by heart and knowing how to cook them is only part of your necessary knowledge for offering a successful dinner—you must also know how to prepare the menu! You have to consider the general preferences of invited guests, the facilities and equipment in your kitchen, and the time allowed for you to cook, yet join them as host or hostess.

Cooking is a challenge, especially if you dare to follow the unwritten rules in the Chinese way. Light and delicate dishes should go first, followed by dishes with heavy and strong seasoning. Since a Chinese dinner consists of many courses, you also have to think about the color of each course. If possible, arrange the menu with very contrasting color order. Serve a dish with a light color followed by a dark one. A dish without sauce, such as deep-fried, before one which has a plentiful sauce. Dishes are not only planned by seasoning, color, or sauce—you still have texture, shape, and taste to be considered. Furthermore, not only should the principal MEAT never be repeated more than twice, the complements should always be varied as well. Then you may expect to enjoy a dinner instead of merely eating a meal. Your chances of enjoying an excellent Chinese dinner will be greater in your own home than in any one of the millions of Chinese restaurants around the world. Sounds incredible, but it is true. Because a commercial restaurant will never match your willingness to offer a good dinner and you don't concern yourself about the profit, which spoils the WHOLE thing!

A professional cook earns his living by cooking. It does not mean that he can do something which you cannot do. After all, cooking is not like lifting weights—which many of us would find definitely impossible—say, 200 pounds?

The Winemaker's Greedy Wife

Once upon a time there was a winemaker who was an unsuccessful but amicable fellow. One day a man, as shabby as a beggar, asked the winemaker if he would allow him to stay overnight. The winemaker thought this stranger was the kind of traveler who always sought aid from others, so he said, ''Well, if you don't mind, you can stay in my cellar.'' ''May I have some of your wine?'' asked the man, who, although dressed so shabbily, was really a god. The winemaker was rather taken aback by this, yet smilingly said, ''Help yourself, and sweet dreams.'' By the next morning, the stranger was very drunk. Before he left, he staggered up to the winemaker and said ''You certainly don't know how to make wine, but you are a good fellow, so I am going to do you a favor in payment for your hospitality.'' With that, he

walked tipsily to the well, which was the winemaker's only source of water, spat into it, and disappeared as smoke in the morning mist. How disgusting!

The winemaker, needless to say, was angry and shocked by this action. He quickly proceeded to clean up the well with a bucket when, to his amazement, he found that the water in the well had been miraculously transformed into the finest quality wine that he had ever made. Thereafter, the winemaker made a good fortune from the wine in the well and did not have to work as hard as other winemakers.

Several years later, the traveling beggar appeared again in the same small town. He, a god, visited the winemaker's place and this time was met by the winemaker's wife. "How is business?" he asked. "Well, not bad since our well produced wine, but now we have to buy lees to prepare our favorite Drunken Chicken!" replied the wife indignantly.

The god laughed heartily and sang:

"The sky is not so high,
Compared to your greediness—that is really high!
Selling water from a well as wine,
Yet you have 'no lees' in mind!"

Then the god suddenly disappeared and the wine in the well became water again.

"Lee" in English has many meanings for nautical use such as lee-tide, leeway, lee-wind and many others. When this word is pluralized it means the sediment from rice wine formed in the first fermentation. Lees is used in the preparation of many delicious dishes. The most popular one, Drunken Chicken, is used for the example in this tale.

DRUNKEN CHICKEN

Drunken Chicken is an eastern Chinese dish which is rarely found on the menus of most Chinese restaurants around the world, especially in America, as most of these restaurants are run by Cantonese.

To make the classic Drunken Chicken, you will need the Chinese Lees, which is very difficult to obtain in most countries. You might find Japanese Lees under the name of "Sake Kasu" with the English name, "Sake Lees." It has the color of cooked, mashed rice. This variety is mild compared to the Chinese type. Since even the Japanese Lees is hard to find, here is a modified method for you, reader, to try this interesting dish. To complete this information about lees, here is a simple explanation for its handling—if it is obtainable in your area.

The purpose of using less is to let the meat (chicken, pork, or fillet of fish) absorb the aroma of lees. To prevent the meat catching the messy lees, it used to be sewn into a bag of coarse cloth. This can be done more easily by wrapping them in a paper towel. In fact, it acts as a "tea-bag" in the broth where the meat is marinated for another day or so. The following method is much simpler without lees. Of course, that Greedy Wife would not like it, because she was demanding too!

Marinade:
    1/4 cup of dry Vermouth
    3/4 cup of dry white table wine
    1 t. salt

If chicken is used:

Try using the trimmed thigh and leg only. Allow one piece for two servings as this is not a main course. It is served as a cold dish at a banquet.

Method:

Cut the chicken at the joint. Leave it in the marinade overnight, refrigerated.

Poaching:

Use enough water or chicken broth, salted to taste, as soup to cover the entire batch of chicken. Bring to a boil, add the chicken and marinade. Leave over high heat uncovered. When the broth begins to bubble again, reduce the heat to the lowest setting, provided the cooking utensil is a heavy type which holds more heat. For a lighter type vessel, the heat should be one setting higher (the second lowest setting). Keep the heat on for 30 minutes, but do not let the broth boil. Then turn the heat off and leave uncovered for another half-hour. (This timing is for the chicken thigh and leg only).

Second Marinade:

   1/4 cup of dry Vermouth
   3/4 cup of dry white table wine
   1 t. salt
   1 cup broth (used for poaching the chicken)

Method:

Mix ingredients together when the broth is still warm. Drain the poached chicken, rinse quickly under cold tap water, drain again and place the pieces in a bowl. Fill the bowl with enough of the second marinade to cover chicken and leave overnight. When ready to serve, cut the chicken parts to bite size and garnish with some of the second marinade. The left-over broth and marinade can be kept in the freezer for another time.

DRUNKEN PORK:

The belly part of the pork should be used. (Side, or Fresh bacon). Because pork has more fat, the marinade is modified somewhat—
    3/4 cup of dry Vermouth
    1/4 cup of dry white table wine
    2 t. salt

Method:

Cut the pork into 2" cubes and marinate for two nights. Turn the pork occasionally so it will be evenly marinated.

Poaching:

Bring to a boil. Cover and cook at medium heat for 15 minutes. Then turn heat off and let stand for 30 minutes.

Second Marinade:

Follow the chicken recipe.

Serving:

Cut the pork cubes into 1/8″ or thicker slices. The pork's texture should be firm and crunchy, if well prepared.

DRUNKEN FISH:

Use less bony fish,

Method:

Cut the fillet into pieces

Marinade:

Same as for chicken.

Poaching:

Five minutes only.

Second Marinade:

The same as for chicken.

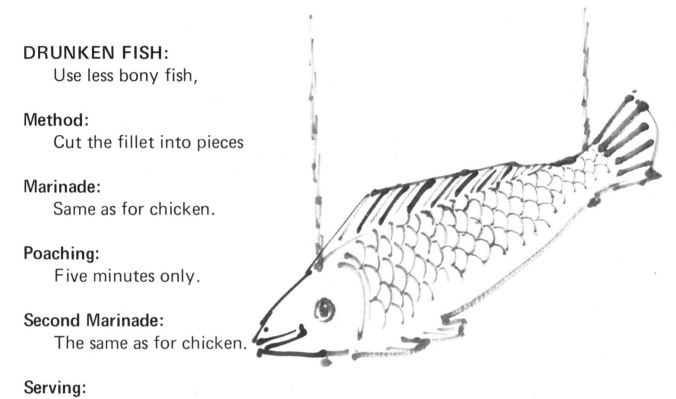

Serving:

As a cold dish, or with hot broth as soup. Warm the prepared fish in the broth before serving. In eastern China, this kind of fish is used for the Hot-pot which is a very delicious variety of Hot-pot cooking.

COOKING TOOLS USED IN CHINESE COOKING

Chinese are very practical people, all tools being designed for functional achievement, not just appearance. A wok is the best shape for all-purpose cooking, especially for deep-frying. The straight-sided deep-frying pot has too many errors in design, as:

  A. It takes a lot of oil to do a deep-frying job.

  B. Its mouth is no larger than the bottom, which gives little room to control the items during the frying.

  C. If the depth of such a pot is not sufficient, you face two other problems:

    (1) Oil will splatter around the cooking area;

    (2) oil will flood out if you dump in too many items at one time.

Chopsticks were invented by Chinese thousands of years ago. What a great invention for simplicity and flexibility in the kitchen, not to mention on the dining table. It is very easy to understand, that with a little bit of practice, you can manage to use a pair of chopsticks as though they were your own fingers, while your fingers could never bear the high heat of oil or of boiling water. To list the uses of chopsticks in the kitchen would take pages. Here are only a few of them to give some ideas:

> For beating eggs; for separating fresh noodles during cooking; to pick up the bunch of noodles in only one move, to pierce meat for checking for doneness; for making more "holes" just before the cooking rice is ready for simmering; to dip into the oil bottle when only a few drops are needed; use them to make a rack so you may stack two dishes to cook in one steamer; etc.; etc.

Chinese cleavers are extremely well designed as a kitchen knife. The short length of blade gives better balance, while a 12" blade is only clumsy to store. Its form is actually rectangular and is two-tools-in-one. Cut the food with the cutting edge, carry the cut food on the blunt square suface—it is a scraper and knife at the same time. Must you cook a French meal with a French Chef's knife **plus** a scraper?

To mash garlic, you don't need two hands to do the job, as the rectangular blade can hardly miss the tiny clove of garlic. By hitting right on the garlic, with a slightly diagonal movement toward yourself, the garlic can be completely mashed in one blow. Its upper blunt edge is very useful as a pounder for tenderizing a piece of meat. Furthermore, a Chinese cleaver will not cost you so much to own. A knife is merely a very ordinary cooking tool, much as a pen is for writing. An expensive pen does not help you become a better writer. Do you agree?

The Chinese Chopping Block is as much required by the knife, as the flying trapeze artist needs a good catcher, or think what would happen! If any non-Chinese cuisine is a handicap to Chinese cooking, perhaps it started by wrongly designing the cooking tools. The block should never be too hard in texture as this will hurt the cutting edge of the cleaver. The round shape will never permit you to cut constantly at the same position nor allow a dent to form in the middle so that eventually even the sharpest knife does not work properly. When you need to cut some meat that has strong bones, a Chinese chopping block can stand heavy blows. Because it is made from a cross section, its grains accept the chopping instead of resisting against the sharper knife. This is the same principle as the known slogan: If you cannot lick it, go with it. So the block can survive!

TOOLS

If you want to make a dress you have to decide what you would like to have. Then you decide on your material and the right tools you will need. The right tools are very important for many jobs and activities. When my daughter Linda was eight, we went for a picnic with a group in a camping resort. There was a pond that had many large carp swimming in it. My daughter could not resist her first chance to fish but she had no fishing gear. She found a piece of rope about a yard long. She tied it on a piece of broken broom handle and tried to fish. Of course she had no hook or bait. She didn't catch any fish but she had a lot of fun. One famous man in history fished with bait on a straight-hook. This man didn't care to catch fish but he enjoyed sitting under the willow tree, thinking what he could do for his country.

The Widow

This story took place during the penultimate dynasty of Tsing in Sze-chwan province in the city of Tsung-tu. A beautiful teenage girl married the fourth son of an owner of a lumberyard. The son's name was Chen. The young couple followed the custom of living in the house of the husband's family. However, there were domestic differences, as the brothers argued about the management of the family lumberyard. The third son took his family and moved to Chung-king (a famous Chinese wartime capital during a twentieth-century war). He opened a medicine herb shop and they lived peaceably. Chen and his wife decided to follow the third brother's action to avoid the endless conflict with his other two brothers. He found a job as manager of an oil factory, and the wife remained home as a housewife—as all women did in those days.

One year passed and the husband's young sister could bear no more of her brothers' fighting. After still another quarrel, she left her family and joined Chen and his wife.

The young couple and his sister were very happy. After ten years had passed, Chen died in a disaster during a river trip. He left no material possessions for his young widow and his sister. The widow was an extraordinary beauty, in spite of a birthmark, so people nicknamed her "Ma" (Mark) as an intimate approach without offending the old rule of calling her by her maiden name. Widow Ma's young sister-in-law had many chances to marry, but having lived with the couple for ten years, and after her brother's tragic death, she preferred to stay with Widow Ma.

They were given the opportunity

to go back to the old family lumberyard, but they knew there would still be feuds, so they decided to earn their own living. Since both were skilled in needlework, they thought they could earn their living just by needles, scissors and thread. But things did not work out very well since they lived in a neighborhood of workmen with limited incomes and not many of them could afford to have new suits made. They did small repair jobs for which they didn't charge much. People couldn't pay them more than their fee, as this was considered insulting or showing bad intentions. During that time (about 1895), men were not supposed to give gifts to women without good reason, especially in the case of a young widow and an unmarried girl. The hardness of their life can easily be imagined.

One evening, as the sun was setting, the laborers were on their way home. Chung, an old carpenter, who was fondly known as "Uncle Chung" by all the villagers, was passing by while Madame Ma was collecting her laundry in the yard. He said,

"Hey, how are you, Madame Ma?"

"Oh, I am fine. How are you, Uncle Chung?" she responded. Chung looked content, but weary, as he held his toolbox in one hand, some packages in the other. He paused on the other side of the fence and said,

"Well, grace to heaven, I got two jobs done today."

"How nice!" she said.

"I should say so!" replied Chung. "I repaired shelves and frames for Wong, the bean curd vendor. He paid me and also gave me four freshly-made cakes of bean curd. At butcher Fong's I planed the cutting block, as I do each month, and he gave me two catties (three pounds) of mutton."

"Oh, Uncle Chung, you certainly deserve them," said Madame Ma.

"Do I? I hope I do. I hope you are not teasing me. As you know, I have no one to cook for me. I know how to use my saw, but not a cooking knife. I know how to repair, but I don't know how to season. What am I going to do with this stuff? It makes me angry not to be able to use it."

Madame Ma could only give a smile of pity as she knew he was a bachelor who could not afford to marry and had no cooking knowledge. Suddenly the carpenter had an idea. He said, "Why don't you cook this food for me?"

Since it was a sincere request from Uncle Chung, she agreed and said,

"With the condition that you don't mind my poor cooking, Uncle Chung."

To write more of this story will be unnecessary, except to point out that the thoughtful Uncle Chung did not pay Madame Ma to cook for him. The food was too much for him alone and, of course, he insisted that it be shared with the widow and her only companion, the spinster. It is said that the first one to use a flower in describing a woman did so by inspiration. Few of us have been given inspiration, yet many of us can certainly copy. Since then, many other men in the neighborhood, pretending that they could not cook, purposely brought more food than they needed, so the two women could have enough for themselves. This at least solved the problem of daily meals. Madame Ma was an excellent cook. The following dish is named after her. It is even now well-known as "Madame Ma's Bean Curd."

She became famous for her cooking skill and people brought her not only bean curd and mutton, but many of the daily food necessities, following the same pattern started by the carpenter, Uncle Chung. Her late husband's employer, the oil factory owner, respected these two women very much because they struggled so hard to live decently and independently. He offered them some money to start a restaurant. They hesitated at first, but accepted the money and the idea and became very successful. The profits from a restaurant in a small village were not great; however, their business prospered.

To avoid inevitable gossip, they did not hire any male kitchen hands. Customers brought the raw materials and paid what they liked as there was not a set charge for cooking costs, including serving. Such a legendary restaurant could have existed only in Sze-chwan, a province that was famous for many unusual things. In 1934 and 1935, both the widow and the spinster died.

Their story is a little wistful if we judge them by modern moral standards and customs. They were raised in a now obsolete society, spending their energy and time in such a way as to avoid temptation and earning their living by sweat and countless sorrows.

BEAN CURD

Many people do not appreciate bean curd when they first taste it. My conclusion is that it is a Chinese food that you need to acquire the taste for unless you were raised in China. Almost none of the Chinese youths born overseas like bean curd. In fact, many of them do not even like Chinese cooking! They prefer a hot-dog to a regular meal. But I know a lot of non-Chinese who like bean curd, and I am delighted to have the opportunity to share with you several different cooking methods for bean curds.

Bean curd is made from the "wonderful bean"—the soy bean, and has been eaten in China for thousands of years. It has always been a favorite food item of the Chinese. There are so many ways to cook bean curd that a recipe book devoted entirely to bean curd could be compiled. A very nutritious food, its texture is controlled during the processing by the moisture content. Furthermore, it is prepared in different forms, depending on the cooking method, such as boiling, steaming, simmering or deep frying. Bean curd is so well known in China that many expressions or short verses about it are used in daily conversation, such as:

"An experienced bean curd vendor, his eye is the scale." This was due to the fact that the vendor of bean curd never used a scale, but measured it by judgment. The expression applies to people who judge the difference between right and wrong by experience.

"Having hundreds of plans during the long night--selling the same bean curd in the morning." This refers to a man with a lot of impractical ideas.

"The fighting hero is selling bean curd!" This means a strong man is handling things soft—for example, a famous factory is now offering a poor product!

MADAME MA'S BEAN CURD

Presuming that you are not a professional cook, you probably do not have available the high heat that institutional stoves can generate. Also, most home cooks do not have the skill to jerk a whole batch of meat and bean curd in one movement in order to bring them to a reversed position. Because of these two deterrent factors, let us use the two-pan system. You will have one more pan to be washed, but the cooking time will be shorter and the result will be more reliable. To make sure you can successfully prepare this dish, I suggest you try making just a small quantity.

You will need one small frying pan for minced meat and one even smaller for the bean curd. Mutton, beef, or pork (in the order of preference) can be used for this dish. The original dish was made with mutton. Mutton or pork should be shoulder chops. Top round should be purchased for the minced beef. In the case of the chops, bone the meat first. Since the quantity of meat is very small, try to mince it with a knife. The texture of meat is spoiled when it has been ground, because the grinder is also a squeezer. Cut the meat into very thin strips, then into bite-size, like a small pea. Cut the bean curd (buy the firmer type) into about 1/3" cubes.

Now you need some spices. The original dish used a reddish-purple peppercorn. The ends open like a tiny flower, hence it was named Flower Pepper in China. If you cannot find this ingredient, you may use ground clove and nutmeg in a one-to-one proportion. For our recipe, you need only 1/4 t. of the spice. If procurable, you should have some special hot condiments. In China, the best one is made of fava beans fermented with hot chili pepper. Your second choice is soy bean paste (fermented) mixed with chili pepper. If this is not available, use some dried chilies or chili powder. Most western hot seasonings in paste or sauce form contain vinegar. If so, it should not be used. Let us put this in recipe form for approximately 2 servings.

 2 cakes of bean curd, the firm type, cubed
 3 oz. meat, or one chop will do, minced
 1/2 t. Chinese fermented bean paste or 1/4 t. chili, dry or powdered
 1 clove garlic, mashed
 1 stalk green onion, finely chopped
 1/2 t. salt (Judge this against the size of the bean curd. No exact
   measurement can be given.)
 2 T. soy sauce
 1/3 t. sugar
 1/4 t. flower pepper
 1/2 cup water or unseasoned broth
 1 t. cornstarch for thickening. (This amount should be determined
   during the thickening. See Information in General.)
 1 t. sesame oil for garnishing
 3 T. oil for starting in the following two-pan system

Pan No. 1   Use a small deep saucepan with 1 T. oil. Add the diced bean curd, turning around gently. Keep over medium heat adding 1/4 cup of water and 1/2 t. salt.

Pan No. 2   Use the frying pan. Heat, then add 2 T. oil. Put in the crushed garlic, onions, and the minced meat. Add the rest of the seasoning and cook for about 30 seconds. Pour the contents of Pan No. 2 over the bean curd in Pan No. 1. Add the rest of the water and turn the heat high to bring it to a boil. As soon as the sauce has decreased by one-half, add the cornstarch, stirring to make it smooth. Garnish with sesame oil and serve.

BEAN CURD WITH EGGS

    2 cakes of bean curd, cut into dice size
    2 eggs, beaten with:
       1 t. of salt
       Pinch of pepper
    1 T. oil
    1 T. water or broth
    1 t. cornstarch

Use 1 T. oil, cook the diced bean curd first for 2 minutes, turning around for even browning. Add 1/3 cup water or broth and 1/2 t. salt. Cook until the water is reduced to very little. Add the beaten eggs to the batch of bean curd. Let the eggs set, pushing the entire batch from side to opposite side several times, so the uncooked portion of the eggs will get into the center where the heat is at its highest. Serve when the eggs are set.

POACHED BEAN CURD WITH STUFFING OF FISH MEAT

    2 cakes of bean curd, cut into eight triangles (Make 2 cross-cuts from
       corner to corner of the bean curd square.)
    2 oz. fish meat, or minced shrimps
    1 oz. minced pork
    1 t. salt
    Pinch of pepper
    1 stalk green onion, finely chopped

Mix these together for stuffing. Cut the longest side of the triangles of bean curd with a small knife, so it forms a slit. Be careful not to reach the edge.

Now pinch the two points—forming a tiny empty space where the stuffing can be inserted with a blunt knife. Bring broth to a boil. The quantity should be very much more than needed to cover the bean curd during the poaching. Barely covering with broth will not have sufficient heat to poach the dish. Immerse the stuffed bean curd triangles in the broth. Leave them set without any heat under the cooking utensil for 10 minutes. Using a slotted spoon, pick the bean curds out. Serve with a light garnish of light soy sauce and a few drops of sesame oil. The broth can be used for soup, de-greasing it before serving.

USING BEAN CURD IN FANCY COOKING

Meat ball of any kind of recipe will be improved by mixing 1/4 part of mashed bean curd. It is almost impossible to detect the taste of bean curd, but the texture will be very much improved, also it cuts down the greasiness of meat.

Freeze the bean curd up to certain degree will change its texture into spongy. The timing must be found out by several checking. Because if it is overdone, the bean curd will be flaky. You may place the bean curd in a container cover with water. When the water turns as ice, it is about the right time to bring it out from freezer.

Cut them into domino size, its spongy texture will absorb any kind of seasoning deeply in few minutes of cooking.

This kind of bean curd is better to be used for stew or cooked in soup of strong seasoning.

Because its natural softness, bean curd can never be cut into thin strips. But you can re-process the soft bean curd (the firmer type) into hard pressed type.

Place the whole bean curd in a pot cover with water, bring it to a boil. Drain and wrap the boiled bean curd in a cloth neatly. Place it on something flat such as a cutting board, then another piece of board on top with some weight, say 5 lbs. Leave it for hours or overnight, the bean curd will be firmer enough to be cut into thin strips for what ever Chinese-frying dish.

A Complaining Guest

Around 500 B.C., during the Warring States dynasty, there were four noblemen who were famous for their hospitality to strangers. They were very generous and offered their guests lavish meals and lodging. However, there were good reasons for such generosity. The four noblemen were extremely ambitious and wanted to create a powerful political party.

One of the noblemen was named Man Song Chuen. Fung Yuen, a stranger, asked Man Song Chuen if he could join his party. He was welcomed and treated as anyone else. Days later, Fung sang to himself: "When will it be true? A coach with a horse to pull?" The nobleman heard Fung's song and immediately, a carriage was ordered to serve Fung.

Several days later, Fung sang again: "When will it be true? A fish dish included in my food?" The nobleman heard this song and ordered fish to be served.

Before long, other followers became irritated with Fung's endless complaints. However, Man Song Chuen patiently accepted all these complaints and willingly fulfilled Fong's wishes.

One day, Man Song Chuen got into trouble politically and he was forced to flee to avoid capture by his enemies. The nobleman and his party left in a great hurry and traveled day and night to a destination in another province where they had a chance for survival. They were only slightly ahead of their pursuing enemies when they reached a fort. Alas, persons were only allowed to enter the fort after the cocks started to crow. The gate was closed when the sun had set. This was the ancient method of keeping time. The nobleman's party arrived several hours before it was time for the cocks to crow, thus there was a great danger that his enemies would reach him before the gate was opened. A fort was always constructed in a location where the only way through was the gate, so there was no alternate route for the party to take. Therefore, the party led by Man Song Chuen was in a helpless situation.

No one could offer a solution. Then Fung Yuen, the complainer, offered to help by imitating a crowing cock. After several attempts, some of the cocks inside the fort responded. He continued to imitate the song until all the nearby cocks were crowing. At last, the guards of the fort were awakened. They opened the gate, and the fleeing party passed through and went on their way.

This is a famous traditional story. The only touch I have added is the Ginger Sauce, which I presume Fung Yuen would have liked. I think part of the merit should go to the cook who served the nice fish dish or Fung Yuen might have left the party much earlier. In which case they would have had trouble in passing the gates of the fort without Fung's ability to mimic the cock's crow!

FILET OF SOLE WITH HOT GINGER SAUCE:

8 oz. filet of sole
1 whole egg plus one yolk slightly beaten
1/2 cup all purpose flour in a saucer

Cut the filet in pieces of 1 x 2 inches or 3/4'' squares

Season with:

1/2 t. salt
1 t. cooking wine
1 pinch of pepper

Dust the seasoned filet with flour, dip them in beaten eggs then roll in flour again.

Deep-frying: F. 325 degrees about 30 to 60 seconds. Keep warm aside.

Sauce: in real practicing the sauce should be ready before the fish has been fried.

> 1 T. finely chopped fresh ginger root
> 1 clove garlic mashed
> 1/4 cup chopped celery
> 1/4 cup chopped onions
> 1/4 cup chopped green or red pepper
> 1/4 cup chopped tomato

Use 2 T. oil and brown the above ingredients for 2 minutes. Add in one cup of water with the following:

> 1 T. ketchup
> 2 T. soy sauce
> 2 t. sugar
> 1 t. sesame oil

Simmer without a lid for 5 minutes. Lay the fried fish in plate, pour on the sauce to cover and serve.

Hot chili powder or paste may be added optionally.

The Thunder God and the Lightning Goddess

To survive, we need food, and rice is one of the principal foods for the Chinese. In ancient times, rice was very difficult to cultivate, much more so than any other food. For this reason, rice was always held in high esteem as one of the most precious items. As children, we were taught not to let even a single grain drop on the floor during our meals. In order to impress us with the seriousness of waste, parents told us that it was very sinful. To dramatize and support this teaching, they told us tales.

One of these tales said that in the beginning there was only thunder, no lightening. The Thunder God searched for sinful men in the world. Minor sins would be judged after death, while the serious ones would be punished on the spot by the sinful man being hit with a thunderbolt. The Thunder God had a list of sins and the worst sin of all was not loving your mother. Cheating in business was also on his list. Alas, if this were true there would be thunderbolts every moment at this time of writing.

One day, the Thunder God saw a man throw something which looked like rice into a trash can. The Thunder God was so angry that he at once hit the man with a thunderbolt. In actual fact, the man had been cooking winter-melon, the seeds of which are white and resemble rice but are inedible. When the Thunder God realized his mistake, he reported it to a superior God. From then on, the Thunder God was ordered to work with the Lightning Goddess. The Lightning Goddess would first light the spot with a bright lightning, which came from a mirror of lightning, then the sin could be clearly judged.

From then on, no more innocent people were punished. We were told that the Thunder God used a giant pin which he aimed at the sinful man and then hit the pin with a hammer, directing a thunderbolt to the sinful man. As can be imagined, no one could survive such a blow! Also, as children, we were assured that we need not be afraid of thunder if we had not committed any sin. So, at the first clap of thunder, our first thought was—did we love our mother?

RAINBOW RICE

Rainbow rice was so named by me because it has seven ingredients and has been proven successful by many people of different nationalities. In the Chinese way, rice is normally cooked without seasoning. To serve rice as a dish, we have many different combinations of meats, etc. In non-Chinese cooking, there are also many combinations of rice with meats, etc. The main difference is that Chinese use pre-cooked rice while the others cook the rice with seasoning and complements at the same time. The following recipe will need to be changed for those who are not allowed to eat shrimps or pork for religious or other reasons. In that case, just omit the shrimps and substitute ground beef, diced cooked chicken, sausage or salami made of pure beef, for the pork.

A book could be compiled on the numerous recipes for Chinese rice dishes, but I selected the following one for inclusion in this book.

SHRIMP: You might only be able to obtain them already cooked. This is all right, but do not use canned shrimp. It is best to use fresh or frozen prawns. Shell them, cut into halves, devein and wash them. Soak, dry, and dice.

EGG: Allow one lightly beaten per serving.

RICE: Never use too much water in cooking the rice for the dish. The rice should be firm and loose. Cold rice is even better. Break the lumps apart with your fingers before cooking this dish to save yourself effort during the cooking operation.

HAM: Use a piece of ham steak, cut into cubes (dice-size).

FROZEN PEAS & CARROTS: The carrots should be in pea-size to match the other ingredients. You can cut carrot rings into pea-size.

GREEN ONIONS: These should be cut into bits.

You may check your ingredients: Rice, eggs, ham, shrimp, green peas, carrots and green onions. A total of seven in various colors—thus the name "Rainbow Rice." Now, for a few hints. You have three choices of cookware. The best is a wok since it is the easiest to turn the rice in and it traps the oil and prevents it from spattering; however, either a deep skillet or a fry-pan is usable. You must use a cooking spoon to stir the food. To turn the ingredients in the skillet, you should jerk the skillet. Regardless of your choice of cookware, you can remove lumps from rice by pressing lightly with a potato masher. This simple operation can loosen rice lumps in seconds, but never press down to the bottom of the cookware. The heat should be at its highest during the entire cooking process. The guiding principle should be two tablespoons of oil per serving to approximately one cup of pre-cooked rice. Use one egg per portion or two eggs per three portions.

PROPORTIONS OF INGREDIENTS PLUS TIMING GUIDE—IN ORDER OF COOKING

If electric range is used, allow enough time for the elements to become red.

Approx. Time Required	Ingredients	One Portion
30 secs.	Oil—part of the oil will be consumed by the pan no matter the no. of portions. So, for 1 serving, add 1/2 T. more.	1 1/2 T.
60 secs.	Shrimps	1 heaping T. of small cooked shrimp, or 2 un-cooked prawns, shelled and deveined, cut in halves and then into small pieces.
30 secs.	Eggs	1 egg
60 secs.	Rice (pre-cooked)	1 cup if served with other course, or more
15 secs.	Peas, frozen	1 Tablespoon
5 secs.	Salt	1 Tablespoon
10 secs.	Ham	1" sq. of ham-steak thickness

Approx. Time Required	Ingredients	One Portion
Cook at the same time as the peas	Carrots, frozen	1 Tablespoon
15 secs.	Green onions	1 stalk
15 secs.	You will need no more than 1 T. of broth or water, if the rice is little dry.	
15 secs.	Light soy sauce	1 t.
15 secs.	White pepper	A pinch

When the rice is put into the pan, if you are using a wok, turn the batch with a spatula so the rice is underneath, bringing the eggs and shrimp on top. This prevents the eggs and shrimp being overcooked. The rice does not need to be stirred during the first 20 seconds of cooking, since it needs that long to heat up. After that, you have to stir the rice or mash the lumps. Once you start to stir, you should do so continuously until the dish is ready. Just a gentle stirring is enough. For large portions of ten to twenty servings, cook in two, three, or four batches and keep them in a warm oven. When the last batch is done, mix them all together again. This is a very handy dish for a large group.

The time indicated in seconds is only a guide to give you the understanding that the entire dish can be cooked in less than five minutes. Don't you think it is great to have a dish ready in such a short time? And it is a delicious one! The time refers, of course, to one portion. The time will be longer to prepare several servings, but it does not mean that you will need fifty minutes to prepare for ten people. For a quantity of 10 servings, you might need 20 minutes.

INFORMATION IN GENERAL:

This section groups information with explanations which you need to remember.

Parts:	To use "part" as a measurement, will make it easy for you to work out the required amount. This simply means you use whatever size of measurement which fits your situation.
Oil:	Only peanut oil is recommended. One famous brand of cooking oil uses cotton seed oil in their vegetable oil, which gives it an objectionable aroma. Read the fine print on the label. One brand of corn oil has isopropyl citrate and methyl silicone. It helps the keeping quality—only!
Sesame Oil:	This is easily obtained through your Chinese grocery store. Use at the end of the cooking period, just before serving. Its purpose is to add a touch of Chinese aroma. You need only a few drops or up to 1 t. per portion of the dish.
Cornstarch:	When thickening the sauce, you can hardly guess the amount required. The only way is to mix some cornstarch with some cold water, about a 1 to 3 proportion. When adding, you must first stir the cornstarch, mixing well, and also stir the sauce. Chinese use many different kinds of starch but cornstarch is more available and this should be well-cooked contrary to someone teaching "Secrets of Cooking."
White pepper powder:	Chinese use only this variety for its lack of color. Let's not argue the slight difference of aroma of black pepper. It is true that freshly ground pepper is sharper, but for professional cooks with many orders, this would be too much trouble. If you grind the pepper hours ahead, you have already lost the aroma, so Chinese prefer to use the white ground pepper. Used in a pure white dish such as chicken breasts, the black pepper is very ugly. Those chefs who insist on black pepper may be heavy smokers. By using black pepper, they don't have to worry if their cigarette ash is carelessly dropped in the food. They can always say—"Oh, that is black pepper!"
Soy Sauce:	Use only the light-colored variety for cooking in general. The darker color soy sauce is only to be used for stew or any dish in which darker color is expected.

Portion of a dish:	A portion varies according to the native land of the cook. There is no rule to follow. However, a normal dinner plate, filled with food in a heap, is about the volume for a single person's consumption. Thus, for a three course dinner for six persons, the volume of each dish should be doubled. This is only a guide for family cooking. If you check this suggestion with most Chinese restaurants, especially those which offer a fixed menu of four to seven courses, you will be disappointed to find that if you put all the seven portions together, there will not be more than two dinner platesful of food.
Sugar:	Always remember—sugar is not for sweetening, except in a few dishes such as Sweet and Sour. A small amount of sugar can blend and harmonize the flavors of any dish; therefore, you must be careful not to over-use it.
Salt:	This is the most important seasoning in all kinds of cooking. If it is rightly used, even a poorly cooked dish will be acceptable, and a properly cooked dish will be unforgetable. The only rule in using it is—use less; adjust by tasting. Salt in cooking is too little to be measured precisely, while sugar used in baking a cake allows a large margin for error. Understanding such a simple explanation will make you a better than average cook.
Vinegar:	Always use red wine vinegar in Chinese cooking. When vinegar is cooked at high heat, the longer cooking will weaken its citric taste giving a delightful milder flavor. That is why, for a Sweet and Sour dish, the sauce should be simmered for a while, about five or ten minutes.
MSG:	Thus far, no manufacturer has dared to teach users about the correct amount of MSG to add to a dish. If they taught the right way, they would worry about the drop in consumer use and, as a result, a drop in sales. But their lack of frankness (and greed?) is a double-edged knife. Too many times, owing to excessive use, people reject the MSG for the resulting objectionable effect. The simplest way to use MSG is to buy the shaker package, turn the top opening to expose only one or two holes, instead of a dozen. When MSG is not over-used, the effect is wonderful.

The Youth With White Robe

Once upon a time, there was a young man whose hobby was raising pigeons of various breeds. He was wealthy, but he wanted to get into a higher society. Thus it was very natural that he tried to meet and associate with noblemen.

One day he visited a nobleman to chat and get acquainted. During the casual conversation, the young man mentioned that he was fond of pigeons. The nobleman said that he too liked BIRDS.

Therefore, the next day, the young man asked his wife to select the best pair of white pigeons from his flock as a gift to the nobleman. Several days later, the young man visited the nobleman again. The young man waited impatiently for his host to mention the gift, but he did not do so. At last, the anxious young man asked the nobleman about the pair of pigeons he had sent him days before. The nobleman suddenly recalled the event and said "Oh, yes! I liked them very much. They were very delicious indeed!"

The young man was stunned and speechless, because the pair of pigeons were of a rare breed and, alas, the nobleman's cook had prepared them as ordinary wild birds!

The young couple was very sad. That night the wife dreamed about one very handsome youth wearing a white robe who scolded her, "You don't deserve to have my sisters and brothers in your possession!"

Suddenly the wife was awakened by the noise of their hundreds of breeding pigeons—flying away!

DEEP-FRIED SQUAB

This dish is usually not prepared successfully in family kitchens for lack of the professional touch required for preparing this dish. It is actually a very simple and clever method of pre-cooking squabs or similar birds—even young chicken.

To start, you need a lesson in looo. Here is a revised page from THE WOK, a Chinese cookbook, which I wrote in 1970. Basically, the looo is a method of storing, in liquid form, subtle spices and food essences. Each person uses a different amount or type of spice so that no two looo are quite the same. Also, the food essences vary according to the age and frequency of use.

An old tradition exists among Chinese restaurateurs, that when a friend is opening up a new restaurant, those who have been in the food business long ago will send some of their own personally developed looo with their compliments so that the new restaurateur will be able to have his loooed dishes up to standard. By sharing their looo with new people, the older generation assures the continuance of this pleasant cooking art. Some owners, as a matter of fact, boast that their looo are hundreds of years old—which is possibly true. How nice are old time folks!

Looo stands for the name of the batch of liquid, which has been explained, but it also means the cooking method in which—if strictly adhered to, the meat should be first poached in plain water or broth. It is then drained and immersed in the looo overnight so it will absorb the seasoning and spices. It sounds as though the looo is a marinade. The difference is that marinade is usually cold and is to be used only for raw meat, while looo is an everlasting batch of seasoning in liquid form and only cooked meat is to be immersed in it and always at a warm temperature. For most family use, only a quart of the looo will be needed, which gives little trouble to freeze in a proper container for further use. Here is the recipe for a quart of looo:

>   2 cups chicken broth (Use only homemade broth without any other
>   seasoning, or use water rather than broth sold at the market.)
>   1 cup dark soy sauce
>   3 T. sugar (preferably rock sugar)
>   1 slice ginger root
>   3 green onions (use only the white part)
>   One 1" stick of cinnamon
>   1 whole star anise
>   1 t. fennel
>   salt to taste (it should be on the salty side)
>   1 cup of dry white table wine

For the squab: Bring the looo to a boil, immerse the squab for poaching as mentioned in the recipe for Drunken Chicken—15 minutes will do, because you are going to deep-fry it again. Drain, and hang it in a windy place. Brush with a coat of the following mixture for crispy texture and golden brown color of the skin:

>   1 T. of honey
>   2 T. of red vinegar (no essence mixed)
>   1 t. of cornstarch.

Normally it takes hours if no artificial wind is applied.

Deep-frying: This is now an easy task, since the squab is already partly cooked. You need enough oil but it is not necessary to cover the whole squab. By turning the squab often, you can easily obtain the golden brown color, while the meat is cooked and remains juicy. The temperature of the oil should be maintained at about 340 degrees.

The Convoy of Treasures

This story is a famous part of a great Chinese novel which has been translated into English under several different titles, including **Water Margin** and **All Men Are Brothers.** Hundreds of years ago, this book was once banned because it had tales of 108 rebels revolting against the government, but almost all Chinese read or hear this exciting story many times in their youth. The tale told here is partially based on a stage show version.

Time: S'ung Dynasty

Weather: A hot summer day

Location: Black Pine Woods—a forest along the route to the Capital.

Principals: An officer leading a troop carrying treasures for a noble's birthday celebration. The officer is a very serious man nicknamed "Blue Face Animal."

Rebels: About ten men. One pretending to be a wine vendor, the others posing as traveling date merchants carrying their goods in wagons.

Situation: It is a hot summer day and the soldiers are very tired. They wanted to pause for a rest in the Black Pine Woods, but their Commanding Officer thought the location too dangerous, as bandits were more likely to attack in such areas. However, he relents, as his soldiers pleaded to stop because they had been carrying the heavy treasures since early morning and are now exhausted.

While they are resting in the shady woods, a wine vendor arrives. He is a skillful thief nicknamed the "Daytime Rat." Since rats steal food at night, a "Daytime Rat" means a rat who dares to come out even in the daytime. This nickname describes his skill as a thief. He carries two casks of wine in the Chinese way, with a pole on his shoulders.

He slows his steps and sings:

> **"Red sun is burning as fire,**
> **Dreary plants in field half-die!**
> **Miserable farmers sweated tire,**
> **Dandies are discussing hair-dye!"**

(The original line was "Nobles are waving fans!" It is rather difficult to interpret the Chinese meaning of "waving fans." It should express the idea that these nobles were relaxing with waving fans. Hopefully, the modified verses express the thought in a way that you may better understand.)

When the wine vendor reaches the top of the hill where the troops are, everyone is tempted to have a "ladle of wine" (the market measurement of wine), except the Commanding Officer. The Blue Face Animal knows quite well that alcohol causes one to sweat, which lowers the body temperature in hot weather, but he is very cautious as it is well-known that bandits sometimes use wine to dope their victims. Who can be sure that this vendor is not one of them? So he denies their request.

An order is an order, so it must be obeyed. The vendor, who overhears what his prospective buyers are discussing, says nothing, but gives an inscrutable smile and starts to leave.

In the meantime, some date merchants arrive with several wagons. When they meet the wine vendor, it is as though a herd of thirsty horses found a fountain in the desert. They rush to the vendor and ask for wine.

"No, I am not going to serve you. The wine is doped," says the vendor. "Are you telling the truth? Come on, let us have some wine!" cry the thirsty merchants. "Aren't you afraid that the wine is doped?" retorts the vendor, "otherwise I would have sold it l-o-n-g before you fellows got here. See the soldiers over there—they said I am selling doped wine so I had better find another location." "Come on", say the date merchants, "We did not say so. Anyway, no vendor would be foolish enough to confess that his wine is doped. Only such a stubborn vendor as you would refuse a sale. Serve us, p-l-e-a-s-e!"

So the wine vendor, to prove that the suspicions of the soldiers are unfounded, agrees and starts to serve wine. The merchants surround him and use ladles to dip wine from one of the casks. While he is tallying the number of ladles he has sold, one of the date merchants opens the wagon and brings out some dates to eat with the wine. They enjoy their wine and dates and in a short time the first cask of wine is consumed. They start to drink from the second cask, but stop after several ladles and say that they have drunk enough. While one of the older merchants is counting the silver to pay the vendor, one of the younger men approaches with a ladle and says, "Hey, you've made a big sale, you've got to let me have one more ladle as a bonus." Without the vendor's consent, the young man goes over to the second cask and slowly dips out a ladle of wine. "You are just greedy!" says the vendor. With great anger and a determined expression, he grasps the ladle when it is just about to leave the cask. "I am sorry," says the older man who paid the vendor. He turns to his companion and says "You should not do that. The wine is very good and the price is reasonable. If you want more, let us pay for it." "Well, actually, I have had enough," answers the young man. "If you do not think we deserve a bonus, what you say goes."

The date merchants and the wine vendor prepare to leave. In the meanwhile, some of the troops who have seen everything with their own eyes, murmur about the suspicions of the Commanding Officer. At last they complain to him about his denial of permission to drink wine on such a hot summer day. The officer relents somewhat. He does not say anything, but the troops take this as a silent consent, so the troopers go to the wine vendor.

"No, no! Your Commanding Officer said this wine is doped!" says the vendor. After such a simple and forthright answer, the soldiers are at a loss for a reply. Then the nice older man, who settled the dispute between the vendor and his greedy companion, comes over to act as a peacemaker again. He says to the wine vendor, "Vendor, why be so heartless? Why torture these poor fellows? Forget this nonsense. Serve them and then be off."

The vendor says nothing, but his manner indicates that the wine is for sale. Finally, he starts to serve the wine to the thirsty soldiers, who invite their Commanding Officer to drink with them.

Minutes later, all the soldiers are doped. Helplessly, they watch the date merchants transfer the treasures to their wagons and then disappear.

In fact, both casks of wine were good in the beginning. When the young man who pretended to be greedy was not allowed one extra ladle as a bonus, he secretly added the dope to the wine!

WINE WITH CHINESE MEALS

Chinese wines are not very pleasing to westerners. I always recommend only dry white wine as table wine for a Chinese meal. Don't follow the general rule that white wine "goes" with white meat and red wine "goes" with dark meat. This does not work with Chinese food. I have seen hostesses insist on serving Chinese wine with a Chinese meal. This adds a Chinese touch, but I doubt if the guests enjoy it since westerners are not accustomed to its very different taste.

Chinese never chill wine. To the contrary, they warm it to about body temperature. I think the Chinese rule is more accurate as room temperature varies, while the body temperature has the same constant warmth.

For cooking, use Chinese Yellow Wine, which is made of rice in the Chekiang province. It is the best for general purposes. In fact, wine is not costly in Chinese cooking as we use it only in small quantities. Many times, it is used only just before a dish is served. Just a few drops of wine gives enough aroma. In European cooking, you might need a bottle of wine for a stew. You can try to use only a spoonful in broth during the simmering period. Then add another spoonful just before serving. This will use much less, yet the dish has enough taste of wine. After an hour-long simmering, the aroma of the wine has been mostly lost in evaporation.

Strong varieties of cooking wine are used in China. This is generally for a special purpose. For instance, if you marinate fatty pork in such a wine, its texture will be firmer. When this cooking method is used, vodka can be substituted for the Chinese wine. Neither gin or bourbon are desirable, because of their strong taste, but Scotch is acceptable for Chinese cooking. Meat for roasting or stewing can always be improved with some Scotch.

CHINESE AND WINE

It was recorded that when the first batch of wine in China was presented to the ruler, Emperor Shun, in the year 2000 B.C., he said, "Some day a nation will be destroyed by this stuff!" Seemingly the Emperor was too modest in making such a prediction.

Wine has been commented on many times in Chinese history, and hundreds of creative, sentimental and immaginative poets have dedicated themselves to compose these impressive poems, with modifications to suit English rhyme. One goes like this:

Among the bushes of flowers, only a cup I own.
Without even one companion, I am sipping alone.
Raising my hand to invite the moon, standing near a tree,
With my shadow, moon and me, we are three.

It seems like whenever Chinese have wine, they like to sing a song or recite a poem. Wine is used for celebrating, drowning sorrow, remembering a parting, and almost for every occasion.

Morning mist set the dust while we are still lingering.
Remember in this inn, with willow trees green.
Please finish another cup of wine with me,
You are leaving westward, no more old pals such as we!

The above is a modified famous parting poem, and the last verse should be sung three time repeatedly. It was quite natural, that parting was a sad event. Like the famous Romeo when he was leaving Juliet, Romeo ended his saying with: . . . so I keep on saying until tomorrow!

COLOR, AROMA, AND TASTE OF A DISH

Chinese have long established the three qualifications for a well prepared dish, and the order was so logically arranged. When a dish is brought to the table, you will notice its color first. A fresh and contrasting color naturally opens your appetite. Then, when you are going to carry the food to your mouth, your nose will catch its aroma. If the aroma suits your fondness, your mouth certainly will water. Now, it is the moment that you expect the seasoning and texture to be correctly done. Then you will enjoy this dish heartily.

It is really simple if we don't have to consider all three qualifications at the same time. For instance, tomato and lettuce freshly tossed look appealing, a curry dish is very aromatic, and strained chicken broth is tasty. But you still have to think to add the right dressing for the salad, the flavor in a curry dish should be well balanced, and something else added to the broth to make it more interesting. Bearing in mind that every dish should have these three qualifications, your cooking quality will definitely be very outstanding.

To deal with the three qualifications will take pages and much practice. Here are some outlines:

Color:
Use contrasting complements such as RED peppers, GREEN peas, ORANGE carrot, WHITE Chinese cabbage, PALE YELLOW bamboo shoots, BLACK mushrooms. The variation is plentiful for you to choose.

Aroma:
Garlic, ginger, green onions are used to season the oil. Pepper powder, a bit of wine, and a few drops of sesame oil turn a dish instantly into Chinese flavor. (Use just before serving.)

Taste:
This has no written rule. However, try to create a dish with its own character. Let the chicken broth be mild in saltiness, a stew dish spicy and heavy in seasoning, and sweet and sour dish should be harmonizing.

Is there any question about Chinese cooking being the second best in the world? Who dares to claim to be THE BEST!

The Cock's Egg

Once there was a slow-witted king who was very fond of eggs. He liked all kinds of eggs, so he ordered his cook to serve him eggs of countless variety. One day he ordered the cook to serve him a dish with Cock's Eggs. The king granted the cook three days to find the Cock's Egg or else he would be punished severely. What an Egg-maniac king!

The cook was shocked by such a ridiculous order, but he sadly returned to his home and was asked by his wife what had happened to cause his worrying. After he told his intelligent wife, she laughed, consoled her husband, and told him not to worry but to enjoy the rare chance of a three day vacation. Two days passed.

On the third day, the wife went to report to the king. She said: "Your majesty, I am glad to report to you that it has been indicated to my husband where the Cock's Egg may be obtained and I hope you will enjoy it as much as the many other egg dishes which my husband has served to you. BUT, I beg you, kindly grant him another few days, because he cannot work now owing to the fact that last night he gave birth to twins." "Lie! How is that possible for a man to give birth?" roared the king. Calmly the intelligent wife replied: "If that is true, how could your majesty order my husband to serve you with Cock's Egg?"

The Egg-maniac king laughed and the cook was spared from punishment.

THE JIFFY CHINESE FRIED EGGS

Egg yolk takes a longer time to cook than egg white, therefore, to expect both the white and yolk to cook tenderly is quite a time consuming job, because you must use low heat, or cover with a few drops of water to steam the yolk to the point of doneness you prefer. However, if you don't care too much about its appearance as a conventional fried egg, here is a very

interesting method. When the egg is in the pan, use a pair of chopsticks, cut—by opening the tips apart first, then closing them together as though you were cutting with a pair of scissors—into the yolk. Cut only the center part, this will open a slit, the yolk will flood out and flatten the original yolk into a larger size. If carefully done, it retains the look of a fried egg, only the yolk is now thinner. With this cooking method, you can easily control the texture of egg white and yolk to arrive at the desired point of doneness at the same time.

CHINESE FRIED EGGS (for 2 servings)

        3 eggs
        1 egg-size of water (Use shells to measure)
        1 t. of cornstarch
        1 t. of salt
        1 pinch of pepper
        1/2 t. of soy sauce
        few drops of cooking wine, optional

Beat the above ingredients together, heat the skillet to very hot, add 3 T. of oil. Swirl the oil to coat the cooking area far enough up the sides to accommodate the entire batch of eggs. Pour the eggs into the middle of the pan. Use a cooking tool, such as a large spoon, if you don't have a Chinese cooking ladle. Push the batch from one side to another, letting the uncooked portion run into the center. Unless you prefer it, don't use the continental method by stirring the batch swiftly with a fork. It gives a different kind of texture. Do gently push the batch of eggs as indicated. It makes the cooking easier, faster and the eggs fluffier. That little amount of soy sauce is an excellent color agent. It should add a pleasant color to the egg and a different taste as well. If the batch burns before the eggs are done, cut the amount of soy sauce slightly. In fact, you need only a few drops for a small serving.

CHINESE-FRIED MILK

Follow the cooking method for Chinese-fried Eggs. Of course use the ingredients called for in this dish.

    3 egg whites
    3 egg-sized amounts of milk (use shells to measure)
    2 t. of cornstarch
    1 t. of cooking wine
    2 t. of salt
    1/4 t. of white pepper (don't use black pepper)
    1/2 c. of cooked crab meat
    2 leaves of lettuce

This is a famous Cantonese fancy dish under the name of Milk which puzzles many people because of the impossibility of "frying" milk into a dish. The lettuce is used for lining the Platter. For serving, place the cooked batch on the lettuce, which creates a delicate fancy dish. A fancy dish should never be served in too great a quantity. Diamond miners know this very well, so they keep the supply to a certain level which maintains the value of diamonds. For this dish you need more oil than usual, say 5 T. of oil. It should not be over-cooked, so the appearance will convince the diner that it is MILK. If the consistency is too solid, slightly reduce the amount of cornstarch, or increase the amount of milk. Of course, the margin is very narrow so you should make notes on your experience for future reference.

The Canvas Drum

Drums are usually made with stretched hide, but there was one temple that used canvas instead. Contrary to the custom of locating churches in a central area, Buddhist temples were located in remote areas requiring a long hard journey for worshipers.

One worshiper decided to pay a pledge to a temple built on a high mountain. He tried several times to complete the difficult climb, but was unable to reach the temple and had to turn back each time. One day in town, he met a monk and discussed with him the failures he had encountered in his attempts to reach the temple. The monk said, "Maybe you are not faithful enough." The man replied, "What do you mean? I am definitely sincere and faithful in my desire to pay my pledge." The monk reasoned, "Well, maybe you commit something against Buddha's commandments without being aware of it. For instance, killing any living animal is not allowed, even indirectly." The man replied, "I don't see that this commandment has anything to do with me. I am a strict vegetarian. I don't even eat eggs."

The monk searched for a good reason for the man's inability to complete his pilgrimage to the temple and suddenly noticed that the man was wearing a pair of shoes which were made of hide. So the monk said, "Ah! You are wearing shoes made of hide. This means that you indirectly killed the bull!" The man agreed with his logic and determined to make another attempt to complete the trip to the temple high on the mountain. He would only wear shoes made of fabric, never of hide. He was so content and confident on this trip that he finally paid his pledge.

He started his journey early in the dawn and reached the temple by midday. It was a lovely sunny day and he enjoyed the beautiful view from the top of the mountain. Before leaving, he paid one more visit inside the temple, accompanied by monks, for a midday worship. Suddenly he noticed that the ceremonial drum was made of hide!

This does not complete the tale—but I have to end my tale at this point because both my mother and grandmother were serious Buddhists. They followed the most strict lifelong vegetarian diet, asking only for their gods to bless me, a problematically ill boy. I cannot deny the fact that I am today blessed with good health.

When I was young, I always argued about religions. According to Buddhism, no living things are supposed to be killed; yet in this tale we found a drum made with hide. This caused one particular temple to use a drum made of canvas. Monks wore gowns made of natural silk made from silk worms.

I wondered why they used a wooden fish as one of their musical instruments and another fish-shaped piece of wood for making the sound which announced mealtime. I can never forget this giant fish-shaped piece of wood that hung high above and the cooking monk hit it with a hammer to announce that a meal was ready. I think a triangle of iron does this job nicely, while a badly chipped wooden fish gave me an unforgettably painful memory.

Many of the most famous temples of China are located in West Lake in Check-kiang province. They are truly magnificent; It is only in these kinds of temples that you find the wooden fish I described. West Lake is also famous for lotus roots, used in several recipes selected for this book.

LOTUS ROOT SOUP

1 lb. of lotus root (choose heavy firm one)
   peeled lightly and cut into finger-size sticks.
1 lb. of pork butt, or beef of less expensive cut.
8 cups of water to cover, simmer for one hour.

Meat can be cut into large cubes or thin slices, before or after the soup is done. This is a very pleasing soup of delicate texture and natural slight sweetness in taste. Season with salt before serving. Approximately 1 T. of salt will be required.

Sweet and Sour Lotus Root.

8 oz. of lotus root, peeled, cut into strips of 1/4 inch
   by 1 1/2 inches.
1 t. of salt.
1 T. of vinegar.
1 T. of sugar.
3 T. of oil.

For this dish put all the ingredients in a pot with a little water for moisture and cook until done, about 10 minutes. It is not advisable to cook this dish in an iron utensil such as a wok as it will turn the lotus root a grayish color.

Dear Reader, this is a page without title but several touching notes which I jotted down during the time in writing this book.

Photos of dishes were ordered in two restaurants of their specialties in Hong Kong. Taken by photographer Chan Wan who is an all round artist but a square person in friendship.

Part of these photos were taken by the author, prepared in home kitchen. No identification is necessary. Those badly exposed were by, of course, Gary!

Polly Ko posed most of these photos with her own belongings. She just picked items available.

Three first-time models were involved in these photos. One is a pleasing waiter with a charming lady reporter and a lady who earned a fortune in restaurant business. As they preferred, no name is mentioned to readers.

A special mentioning about Mr. Walter S. W. Lee, the Manager of the well known Toppan Printing Company. Without his patient and professional assistance, this book would never be possible to finish.

one famous newspaper editor occasionally left some blanks without revealing his reason, although he could have filled them easily. However the hidden motive was eventually known by his colleagues. I, as the author, dare not to match such feats. Timidly I have just enough courage to leave this page blank. Believing there are only three persons who know my motive, namely Mike Nelson who artfully did the layout, Beth and Louis Crittenden who painstakingly helped me to finish this book. To them I owe invaluable assistance, to readers an illustration!   Gary Lee

Three Blessing Stars

China never had a religion of her own. The Great Master Confucius was a scholar and philosopher. He never expected people to regard his teachings as a religion. He once said, "Respect the gods and devils but keep them at a distance." Taoism is often misunderstood. The **Book of Morals** was written by Lao Tze before Confucius' time. Not until thousands of years later was it used as a bible of Taoism by a man with many followers, who practiced black magic and claimed to perform miracles. The man used this book because he knew he must have something for his faithful to read as the true word.

As her culture developed over thousands of years, China had many beliefs in order to satisfy spiritual needs. There were many gods—Door-god, Kitchen-god, Sea-god, and Mountain-god are a few examples. The Three Blessing Stars are like the westerners' Zodiac Signs or Houses. Each was thought to have control over our fate. The three stars refer to Happiness, Prosperity, and Longevity. What more could a person desire? We have never had an orthodox picture of Jesus Christ, but fashioned our own likeness of him. The Chinese believe that from carefully looking at one's features one can learn much about the sciences of physiognomy and statistics.

I will now explain the divine order. It is Happiness, Prosperity, and Longevity. In China, the order is from right to left when a sentence is written horizontally, and even though all of us would like to live longer, Happiness is the first choice. The right hand one is Happiness. From comparing his beard with those of the others, you will see that it is much shorter, which means that he is younger. He is dressed very simply and he has a humble expression. This conforms with the western belief that even without a shirt, if one is humble, one can be content—and that is the way to be happy.

The middle one is Prosperity. He wears a hat which is a symbol of high rank. Too few of us can be kings, so the most probable second highest goal to wish for is prosperity.

Prosperity has a longer beard which shows that one can only achieve such a stage when one is middle-aged. Because of his achievement, he wears very luxurious clothes. His belt is studded with jade and he holds an ivory ceremonial ruler in his left hand. Notice his expression. His eyes are somewhat proud. Since he is very high in rank, his robe is embroidered with a design of dragons and clouds which was the symbol only of the few who ruled people.

The old man is Longevity. He is shorter with abnormally long ears, a very prominent forehead, long eyebrows, a white beard, and wrinkled hands. These are the characteristics of men with long life. That very long pole is a Chinese walking-stick. On top is a Peach of Longevity. The deer in front of him is Longevity's companion. This means that he likes wild animals as pets and he has certainly spent most of his time in the wilderness, as you can see that the deer holds a stalk of herb in his mouth. This is the Magic Herb which cures any illness and can only be found in the deep forest of mountains which only a deer can reach.

We Chinese have an expression which says. "Your Three Stars are Shining for You." This means that in you is the perfect combination of goodness. The frequently used "Wish You All the Best" is not very clear in meaning. How can you ask for "All the Best" which could be hundreds of wishes? That would be too excessive to ask of even the generous Almighty. Good wishes are always welcome, so the Chinese have many dishes with the name "Three Stars." Here are several established combinations.

ESTABLISHED COMBINATIONS OF THREE BLESSING STARS:

Cooking method to be used: Chinese-frying, that is, heat a wok or skillet until very hot, add oil, cook.

Order of Cooking:
First cook the complements until 3/4 done. Set aside. Cook the principal until 3/4 done, add the complements, cook until the batch is done, adjust the seasoning and serve. The principal and complements are separated to better control the different times required for perfect cooking.

Cutting:
Try to match them, i.e., all in strips or all in slices.

Proportions:
One-third of each, in volume.

Quantity:
This is dependent upon the number of courses you require. The following amounts are suggested for 2 servings:

8 oz. chicken breast, sliced, marinated in—
- 1 t. salt
- 1/2 t. sugar
- 1/8 t. white pepper
- 1 egg white, unbeaten
- 2 t. cornstarch
- 1 t. peanut oil

Variation I: Chicken breast in slices
- Soaked dried mushrooms (a)
- Bamboo shoots (in can) (b)

Variation II: Chicken breast in slices
- Soaked dried fungus (Cloud ears) (c)
- Snow Peas (d)

a, b, c, and d can be used in any combination. But Chinese cooking has certain unwritten rules; for instance, you should never combine fungus with mushrooms, for their colors are all black and would not provide contrast. The white part of Napa Cabbage can also be used in this dish.

In Strip Form: It is just the same, only the cutting is in strips.

Variation for Serving Strips: You can use a small handful of Mung Bean Threads, or Dried Rice Noodles; deep-fry them in hot oil (350 degrees) and they will take only seconds to burst into a fluffy bunch. Place the fried noodles on a platter, and cook the strips dish, using more than the normal amount of sauce. Thicken it lightly with cornstarch and pour the cooked strips on the deep-fried threads (or noodles), which will absorb the sauce. This is a very elegant, delicious dish of a pleasing color when served.

Variation of Chicken Strips: (Use the same marinade)
1 part of chicken strips, marinated
1 part of cooked bamboo shoots
1 part of cooked ham: Use ham steak to obtain thicker strips to match the chicken strips. Normally, the ham steak is too thick for a strip, so you should cut it in halves first. If this is too difficult for you to do, you may purchase a large slice of whole cooked ham, about 1/8'' thick, or you may use thin slices of cooked ham, using 2 slices as one piece. If you do not separate them, they will adhere together, even after you blend them with the rest of the ingredients. That is, first cook the chicken strips, add the bamboo shoots and then add the ham strips just before serving. Combine the entire batch, gently.

1 part of chicken strips
1 part of cooked ham
1 part of green or red pepper

Ham can never be used as the principal in such a dish, so here is another variation without ham:
1 part of chicken strips
1 part of green pepper
1 part of bamboo shoots.

Vegetarian Variation: (Either in slices or strips)
1 part of soaked dry mushrooms
1 part of cooked bamboo shoots
1 part of snow peas, cut into strips
1 part of Napa Cabbage, the white part only.

Use any three of the above ingredients.

Napa Cabbage is so named because the most famous Chinese Tien-gsing Cabbage is mass-produced in the county of Napa in the state of California. If someone decided to breed the famous German Shepherd dog in Napa, I wonder what they would name it?

THE NUMBER OF RECIPES IN THIS BOOK

On many occassions people have asked, "How many recipes does your book have?" It seems that people think the more the better. I don't agree. I am not only limiting the number of recipes but I am also limiting the number of ingredients used. For instance, we have many different kinds of squash, which I presume would not be mentioned only two or three kinds of fish and left the other hundreds of kinds of fish for other cookbook writers to produce a chart of cooking fish that would be pages long. I confess that I haven't even heard the names of most kinds of fish, but I can assure you, that if you show me a fish, I would probably know how to prepare it. Please don't give me a poisoned fish like the one used in Japan. You need a special license to handle it. In cooking vegetables, consider their shape, texture, and taste. You don't need me to explain things to you item by item. Please use your good sense.

CREATION OF NEW RECIPES

It is very difficult to create a new Chinese recipe because it should be created with some rules and good sense. A famous fashion designer in Los Angeles represented his master creation as being for both sexes. He shaved off the hair of both his male and female models. He himself had ordinary hair and wore a dress in the picture with his models. It would seem that the designer didn't care for his creation. Why didn't he shave his own hair?

I have studied cooking for many years. I have learned many techniques but I have created no more than twelve original dishes. Even some of these few dishes are merely improvements of established recipes. Not everyone will necessarily agree that all of them are improvements of the original recipes. If you allowed me to create a new dish without thinking about rules and good sense, I think I could easily create a new dish every five minutes. If you reward me one drink for each dish I created, after several creations I should need only one minute for each new creation!

HOW LONG DOES IT TAKE TO LEARN THE ART OF SEASONING?

I learned to drive a car in less than ten lessons. My first several weeks were very hard and then it seemed easier and easier. After driving every day for five years I suddenly felt that I could park much better. Since then I have been able to park well. Yet, after almost twenty years of driving, I still have to make a slight adjustment in my parking. The same is true in seasoning. You will be clumsy in the beginning, but you will become much more skilled if you continue to cook. Then someday you will notice that you are doing it much easier and better. If you cook for your grand-daughter's wedding party, you might not be satisfied with your seasoning. Nobody will blame you so don't worry. For such a party, they will even be pleased if you use sugar instead of salt for the chicken broth.

CHECK DISHES BEFORE SERVING

By checking each dish before serving it you have a chance to make corrections if the dish is not perfect. This takes only a few seconds and very little effort. However it can help you produce dishes of better quality.

Sauce   The quanity should be just right. If there is too much, leave some in the kitchen. If there is too little, add in some water.

Taste   Unless you have badly overseasoned your dish you can make some adjustments before serving. Just add some soy sauce or salt if needed.

Smoothness Usually a little bit of oil makes a dish smoother.

Garnishing This improves the appearance and aroma of a dish. Use in small quanities. Only edible garnishing is used in Chinese cooking.

Barbarian's Head

The following tale was recorded in history during the time of The Three Kingdoms, 221-265 A.D. Chinese consider Chu-kuo Liang as a man who never was and never will be surpassed for his wisdom. He was indeed a great man, the most famous strategist in our history. Sun Tze is probably better known to westerners, since his book about military theory has been translated into many languages. However, Chu-kuo Liang was a realist. He left to history hundreds of tales about his intelligence and sophisticated intrigues. I cannot use all of his tales in this book. I can only share the one which relates how he invented our famous steamed buns.

When he was the Commander-in-Chief for the Kingdom Souk, which occupied the present day province of Sze-chwan, Chu-kuo Liang was planning to invade the eastern part of China. He believed that before invading the east, he must first conquer the part of his southern area which was ruled by a barbarian tribe. This plan left us a famous saying: "To avoid any possible back-door bothering." So he brought his troops to the south and fought against the barbarians and their ruler, who was named Man-who.

These barbarians were very strong physically, but were unable to compete with the intelligence of such a great man as Chu-kuo Liang. The first encounter ended quickly with Chu-Kuo Liang defeating Man-who. Man-who said that he did not mind dying, but complained that he had lost the battle because of events beyond his control. Chu-kuo Liang reasoned that it would be useless to kill this ruler without winning the admiration of the tribesmen. Therefore, he freed his prisoner and permitted him to battle again.

Since this is a cookbook, I will save space by telling you that Chu-kuo Liang captured Man-who seven times and each time Man-who had a different excuse for his defeat. By then, of course, Man-who realized that he was definitely not capable of fighting against such a great man. He accepted his

defeat and bravely confessed admiration of his conqueror, promising to order his tribe not to bother the Kingdom Souk. This is a good example of what Sun Tze meant when he said that "Gaining a castle is good, but gaining the admiration of the enemy is magnificent."

Since the war was settled honorably for both sides, Chu-kuo Liang brought his troops back to Kingdom Souk. Man-who accompanied him to the border. They reached a river where, it was believed, a human head had to be sacrificed in order to cross safely. The tribesmen had offered human heads there for many years. They were of the opinion that because so many innocent persons had been killed in battle, ghosts of the slain demanded human heads to appease their anger. The great Chu-kuo Liang had a different point of view. He argued that if you killed someone and offered his head to the ghosts, you might have peace from those ghosts—but what about the sacrificial slaying of **this** innocent man? His ghost would also demand something in return and the problem would be never-ending.

Chu-kuo Liang said that this custom should be changed. It might be true that these ghosts demanded something such as a human's head, so why not let us offer something similar? He gave the order to use dough, stuffed with meat and shaped like a head, to be dumped into the river. His troops crossed the river peacefully, of course, and from that time on, no more human heads were sacrificed. The credit must go to some unknown cook who made the mock head so delicious. Someone "tried it and liked it." Soon everybody

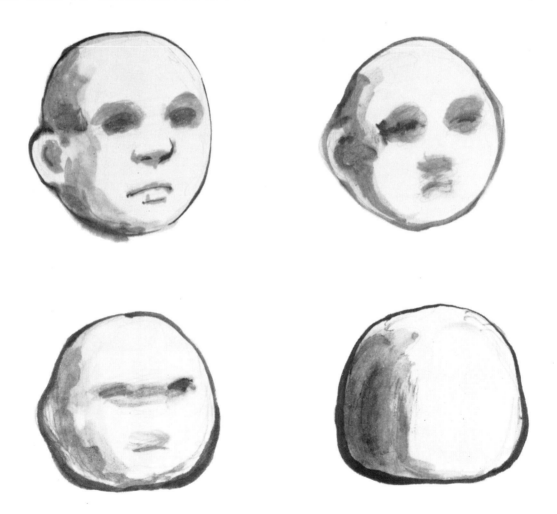

liked the mock head. For practical reasons, its shape was changed into a bun and its size was considerably reduced. The name "Barbarian" implied "uncivilized" so, although the pronunciation remains the same, in writing it now has another character with a more tranquil meaning.

STEAMED BUNS:

Unfermented steamed bun is simple and quick to make, the dough is thin and firm, the size should be smaller than the fermented type. The only thing you need to add in flour is water.

> 2 cups of all purpose flour
> 1 cup of water

Either cold, warm, hot or boiling water can be used to make the dough. Knead it well to a soft consistency.

The temperature plays a big role in this dough. The cold water makes the dough firm while hotter water turns the dough soft. You can choose whichever you would like to use by controlling the temperature of water, or by mixing two batches of dough made with different consistencies.

Fermented Steamed Bun

> 4 cups all purpose flour
> 2 T. lard
> 1/2 cup sugar
> 3/4 regular small cake of yeast
> 1 cup milk

Mix sugar and milk with yeast. Keep aside for 20 minutes. Cut the lard finely into flour and add to milk mixture. Knead roughly, set aside for an hour or more covered in warm place. When the volume has nearly doubled, knead again and let it relax again for another 40 minutes.

The above recipe is Cantonese style, while the Northern style will use much less or no sugar. The result will be same only the latter one tastes slightly sour owing to the yeast was not countered with enough sugar.

General rules in handling of dough

Sifting the flour is not so important as compared to the gentleness in handling the dough. Always knead the dough with gentleness and let the kneaded dough be relaxed.

When you finish the filling and the buns are ready to be steamed, cover and LET it relax once again, say another 15 minutes.

MEAT STUFFING:

> 1 lb. minced pork (or beef, etc.)
> 4 T. soy sauce
> 1 t. sugar
> 2 T. cooking wine
> 1 pinch of pepper powder
> 2 stalks of chopped green onions

This recipe works with ground beef too. In this case, try ordinary onions instead of green onions. Also finely chopped celery can be used in the batch.

When additional volume of vegetables is used the right amount of salt should be increased for adjusting the saltness.

Vegetarian's Bun

This is a very delicious variation. No exact proportions can be defined. However, use the following items according to your taste and availability.

Chinese Cabbage, Watercress, Spinach. Use only one at a time. Chopped finely, sprinkle it with salt, let it breathe and press out the excess moisture. Soaked mushrooms can always be used.

A whole cake of bean curd should be boiled for five minutes. Then it should be wrapped in cloth and place some weight on. Leave, say for five hours. By then it should be firm for cutting.

Hard-cooked scrambled eggs.
Mung Bean Threads, pre-soaked and drained.

Cut EVERYTHING in tiny strips.
More oil should be used in vegetarian's stuffing or it will not taste smooth.

MEASUREMENT OF SHOES (Measurement of Seasoning)

Since seasoning is so important in cooking, this tale was especially chosen to explain the only reliable way to measure seasoning. There once was a man who decided to buy a pair of shoes. On a slip of paper, he jotted down the size taken from a pair of his shoes which were very comfortable. On arrival at the shoe shop, he discovered that he had left the slip of paper behind. He went back to his home to get the paper and again returned to the shop. But it was late—the shop was closed! When he expressed his unhappiness about his futile trips, he was asked, "Why didn't you let the shoes be tried on your feet?" He replied, "No, no! I would rather trust the measurement than my feet."

This tale was written by Han Fei Tze, during Ch'un Chiu 403-221 B.C. Master Han did not write this tale for seasoning in cooking, but it is clear enough that we should trust our taste-buds more than a static measurement which cannot be reliable—especially in the small quantities required for daily cooking.

NOTE: Readers should not confuse cooking with baking. These two are entirely different when measurements are applied.

WHAT COOKING MEANS IN CHINESE

One big mistake that most readers make is not knowing the difference between cooking and baking. Don't think that you can make anything if you have the right recipe. This may be true in making such things as cakes and breads, but this is not true in cooking even a simple dish such as an omelet.

The baker's basic rules can be clearly defined and can be followed with little difficulty. One can follow such rules as pre-heat the oven to a given number of degrees, sift the flour, melt the butter, measure precisely, and don't examine unnecessarily during the baking, etc.

Cooking, especially the Chinese way, is just impossible to define in such a way, as it requires a lot of good sense, judgement, and experience. If you approach cooking as you do baking you will be very disappointed in the results. A good baker can produce hundreds of cakes of a certain kind and nobody can sense any difference. A good cook has no such advantage. In preparing the same dish a hundred times, he is a genius if he can manage eighty percent of them to be of the same quality.

This is the main reason I have written this book. It was not written just to give you recipes from the second page to the last as so many cookbooks do. I do not pretend that cooking is as easy as ABC as many claim. This book is written to help you understand how to cook. Unless you are willing to read and practice carefully, I don't think you will find anything useful in this book—maybe a can-opener will do a better job. I also think that a reasonable amount of effort spent on any job will bring joyful rewards.

THE BEST GROUP OF SECRETS IN COOKING

I notice one interesting characteristic of the art of cooking as compared to the other arts. In painting, for example, you may try as many times as you need to produce a finished piece of art and the length of your life is your time limit. Once you become famous, anything you paint will be kept as a treasure. A modern painter can show you a white piece of paper and call it "Sugar Loves Salt" or call a black piece of paper "Midnight in the Jungle."

A cook is not supposed to cook again and again in order to present you with a satisfactory dish, and he definitely could not give you a dish which you don't like and tell you, "This is a 'Modern Cooking.'"

Once a great sculptor was asked by his students to summarize his artful secrets. The master coldly said, "Just chip away the undesirable part and leave the desirable part!" I agree with him. The secret in cooking is just to buy the right ingredients, cut them accordingly, cook to the right point, and season to taste. Is that all? No, serve them hot, with a good choice of complements, in proper shapes and size of platters, and to the right person.

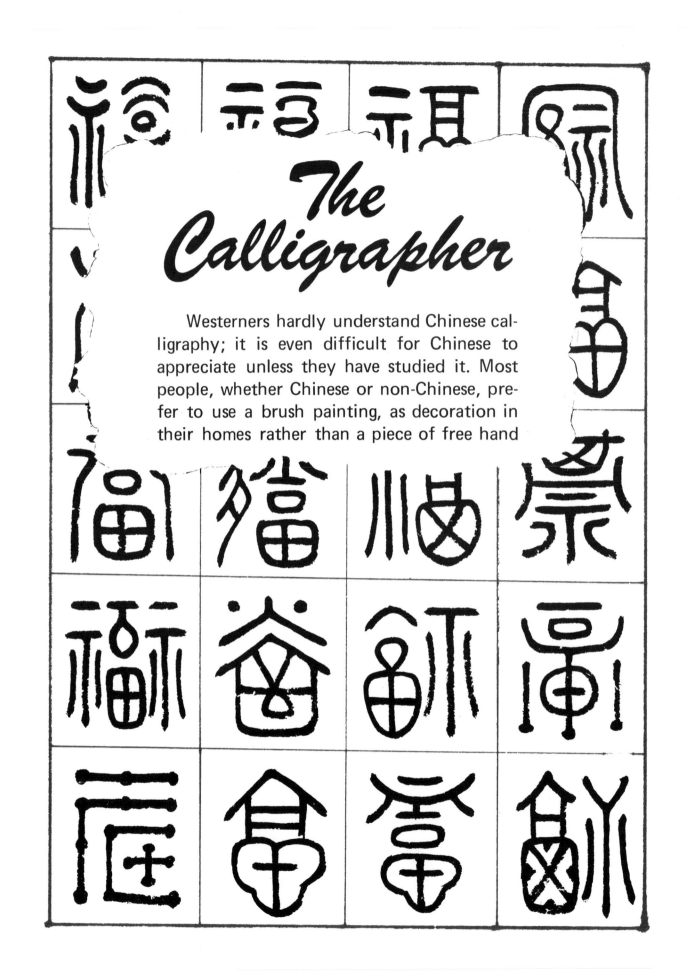

The Calligrapher

Westerners hardly understand Chinese calligraphy; it is even difficult for Chinese to appreciate unless they have studied it. Most people, whether Chinese or non-Chinese, prefer to use a brush painting, as decoration in their homes rather than a piece of free hand calligraphy. A brush painter uses scenes to please viewers, while a calligrapher must have excelled in literature. His poetic verses coupled with his ingenious dexterity in calligraphy allows you to enjoy and respect his work with endless appreciation. You will never have a problem if you hang a painting, but this is not so with calligraphy. Someone might ask you to explain it when you can hardly even read it—much less explain the meaning.

Here is one version of a tale about a calligrapher.

One calligrapher was so famous that he began refusing to write any more. Perhaps he thought that the fewer works he created, the more value they would have. Mass production is definitely not for an artist. The inhabitants in his town needed someone to write a sign for a new building. Even though they only needed three characters, they knew it would be useless to offer money to this famous calligrapher, so they devised a plan to inveigle him into writing them, using his fondness for Stewed Lamb.

After thoroughly formulating their plot at a secret meeting, the people of the town invited the calligrapher to accompany them on a hike in the country. During the long hike, they stopped at a public hall for a lunch break. Everyone was very hungry. Some people were setting the table while others had been busy preparing the lunch before the hiking group arrived and the tempting aroma of Stewed Lamb with five fragrant spices was filling the hall. Umm!

Just before lunch was to be served, one member of the group said "Wow! Tomorrow is the deadline for us to put up the sign for our new building. Let us first finish the sign." In only seconds, others brought the required paper and ink, so he began to write. He started seriously and carefully. When he reached the third character, he suddenly stopped and said "Oh no! I did a bad stroke on the second character. Let me try again." So he tore the paper and started again. The entire group watched him in total silence. This time he confessed, as he was on his second character, that he did not write the first character properly. He insisted on trying again and again until several sheets of paper had been discarded. Meanwhile, the noise of twisting stomachs was nearly audible—the aroma of lamb stew being invisibly tempting to all appetites. The famous calligrapher could not resist any longer.

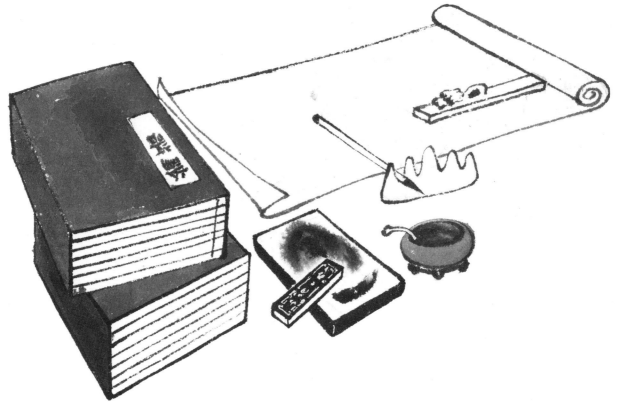

He said "Let me try it for you!" No one disagreed. The man who had written and torn up so many sheets of paper, with a bow, stepped aside politely and quickly. In seconds, the sign was made. Cheating? Yes. In Chinese we say, "A gentleman can always be cheated for his squareness." After all, the motive to cheat him was to have an attractive sign for the town, not just for the inflation of a single person's ego.

LAMB STEW WITH FIVE FRAGRANT SPICES

Ingredients:
> 2 lbs. cracked lamb ribs
> 4 T. soy sauce
> 2 t. honey
> 2 T. oil
> 1/2 c. dry white wine to be added according to directions
> 1/2 t. five fragrant spices

NOTE: The four commonly available spices are: Star Anise, Cinnamon, Cloves, and Nutmeg. If spices are not finely ground, the quantity should be slightly increased as compared to the mentioned 1/2 t. in this recipe. If you cannot obtain these spices through your Chinese grocer, your chance of proper spicing will still be 80% to the good, because at least four of the spices, as mentioned above are available everywhere, the exception being the peppercorn of purple-reddish color. It has an open end like a tiny flower bud, hence its name in Chinese is Flower Pepper. This peppercorn is not too strong (hot), but has a sharp aroma and a very mild, pleasingly bitter taste. Blend the five (or four) spices together and measure 1/2 t.

Since this is a stew, you do not need the best cut of meat. Chops are not only expensive, but their texture is not suitable for stewing. Ribs are recommended. You may crack them in half (not too small), or you may stew them in a single piece. This keeps shrinkage low and the bones add a delicious flavor. You may serve with bones if you prefer to use knives and forks instead of chopsticks.

First, prepare a mixture according to the weight of the lamb. For each pound, you need two tablespoons of soy sauce and one teaspoon of honey.

Coat the pieces with this mixture and brown in oil, uncovered, at high heat. When they begin to sizzle, reduce the heat and cover. The actual timing and heating can only be determined by trial and error, since cookware differs. However, if you do not hear a sizzling sound from the covered vessel, the heat is too low. In that case, increase the heat slightly. The most important thing is to control the moisture content, check them after approximately ten minutes. There should be juices which should be kept to less than 1/2" in depth. If there is excess juice, drain and keep for addition to the stew later. Check every 15 minutes. Because there is so little juice, the upper portion of the meat will be cooked by steaming, so the meat should be turned over periodically.

After an hour, add the pre-drained juice, if any, or some table wine, a few tablespoons at a time. When the bone sticks out about 1/4" from the meat, it is cooked. However, you may test for doneness by tasting. Correct the seasoning. Add 1/2 t. of five fragrant spices. Simmer for five to ten minutes.

This stew differs from others in that there is very little sauce. It should have a prominently sweet taste, yet salty enough with a strong aroma of spices. If you prefer more sauce, as in a conventional stew, then you will have to reduce the amount of honey used. Add more water at the end, after removing the meat. (Why? If the meat was not removed while you added the water and thickened the sauce, the meat would lose its delightful color!) Thicken with cornstarch, return the meat to the sauce, and serve.

Pork Stew with Five Fragrant Spices:

2 lbs. pork butt, cut into 1" cubes

Follow the same directions as for Lamb Stew.

Variations:

Add some bamboo shoots, cut into chunks, during the last 15 minutes of simmering. Volume of bamboo shoots should be about one-half the amount of pork used.

Other Variations:
2 lbs. pork, cubed
8 hard-boiled, shelled eggs (eggs to be added after pork is half-done.)
2 oz. soaked-dried mushrooms for more aroma

Chicken Stew with Five Fragrant Spices:

2 lbs. chicken, thighs and legs, cut into chunks

Follow the same directions as for Lamb Stew. Mushrooms and bamboo shoots can also be added to this dish. However, make more sauce as rice is usually served with this dish.

Beef Stew with Five Fragrant Spices:

2 lbs. beef, brisket
1 lb. turnip, peeled
and cut into chunks

Follow the same directions
as for Lamb Stew.

Extra Sauce:

When the stew is done, remove the meat and/or complements. Add desired amount of water and seasonings. Thicken with cornstarch, blend in the cooked meat and serve. By preparing the sauce in this way, the meat will retain its texture and color.

HOME MADE SALTED PORK WITH TURNIP SOUP

Commercial salted pork is absurdly salty. No, they are cleverly prepared, so the product can be kept longer, and you pay for the excessive weight of salt in the price of pork! Let us make our own.

　　1 t. of salt peter, dissolve it in 1 T. of dry white wine
　　20 t. of salt, mix it with above
　　1 piece of spare ribs, 2 to 5 lbs.

Rub the salt mixture all over the ribs, which should not be washed. Leave it in cold place overnight, preferable windy. If the sunshine is strong, hang the salted ribs under the sun for several hours at a time. Don't let the sun cook the ribs. When it is apparently dry, hang it only in a cold and windy place for several days, then it is ready for use. Another easier method is to have the salted ribs, wrapped in a plastic bag, (after the first overnight left out) place it in the refrigerator at a warmer spot, for several days. Either way, cut the amount of ribs to be used and rinse them with tap water.

Remarks:
For the first method, the ribs should be left whole. For the second method, the ribs may be cut into pieces. For each slice of ribs, (the whole length) will be enough for each cup of water and the resulting soup will be strong enough for. Bring the water and ribs into a boil, simmer for one hour. Since simmering will decrease the amount of water after an hour, some more water may be added to compensate for that lost by evaporation.

During the last 15 minutes of simmering, add in peeled turnips cut in diagonal thick slices, adjust the seasoning before serving.

Remark:
The suggested mixture of salt is only for easy measuring. You use only the required amount of the mixture to completely coat the ribs in curing.

MOCKED BEAN CURD SOUP

There is no such thing as Mocked Bean Curd in China, since readers might live in somewhere that no bean curd is available, this simple dish is very pleasant to satisfy your craving for bean curd, the soft type for soup.

2 eggs
4 eggs-size of water,
    use the half broken
    shells as measurement
1 t. of salt

Place the above beaten mixture in an oiled bowl for steaming. A thermo-controlled electric cooker is helpful in this case. Set the dial at 200 degrees, with an inch of water, and the bowl on a rack. The rack can be anything such as a pair of chop-sticks. The purpose is only to keep the bowl from shaking too much when the water tends to boil. After 15 minutes, the mixture should be firm, counting after the first time the light blinks. Check the firmness with a toothpick as you do for your cakes. Since the exact time varies according to the quantity and type of cooker.

Remarks:

The mentioned 200 degrees is also only a guide. Since not every thermo-control dial is perfectly gauged. Water is supposed to boil at 212 degrees. The suggested 200 means don't let the water come to a boil. If the first try of this batch is longer than 15 minutes, you can be sure that the thermo-dial was not functioning correctly. Then try to set it at 205, or 210 degrees. On the contrary, if the batch is cooked sooner than 15 minutes, or the texture turns spongy, then you should try to set the dial at 195 or less.

When this batch is done, you can simply heat some broth seasoned to taste, scoop the cooked egg mixture with a thin metal spoon, gently into the soup and serve. It is very deceiving as mocked bean curd in soup.

The Honest Cook

Once upon a time, a man had two daughters. The elder daughter was named Fong Yuk, which meant "Square Jade". The younger daughter was named Yuen Chu which meant "Round Pearl". Both of his daughters worked as cooks, serving in the royal kitchen of a king. One day, the daughters were very busy preparing food for a banquet. Dumplings were cooking in a covered pan with very little water to produce steam. The water was carelessly permitted to evaporate and so the bottoms of the dumplings were scorched. This had never happened before.

Each cook in the royal kitchen had a personalized garnish (made from cooked carrots, etc.), each of a different design, which indicated who prepared a certain dish so scores could be given to the cooks. Young Yuen was very frightened, because it was she who had prepared the dumplings. The elder Fong said, "Well, it is too late to prepare another batch. Serve them just as they are. Since we are sisters, you shall also use my garnish and let me share the blame." Just before the dumplings were to be taken from the kitchen, the elder Fong said, "Since we never serve them with scorched bottoms, let us turn the bottoms up. Then the king can see that they are burned before he eats them and he will know we have no intention of deceiving him."

Unexpectedly, the turned-up bottoms of the dumplings were deliciously crisp and the king enjoyed this new variety of dumpling very much. The king ordered that the sisters be rewarded. When the sisters were summoned to the court for rewards and to tell the name of this new dish, the elder Fong was speechless, but the young Yuen was quick-minded about a title for her unplanned culinary success. She replied, "Your Majesty, this is Quo-tik. It is different from ordinary Chio-tze. We let them stick to the pan to form this nice crispy crust."

The king was very satisfied and asked this dish be included in the official menu.

Quo is "pan" and tik is "stick", hence Quo-tik translates into "Pan-stickers."

PAN-STICKERS

Chio-tze is the general name of a kind of dumpling. It can be cooked by boiling in water, steaming, or with a little oil plus water and pan fried until the crust is brown.

Different doughs are required for various cooking methods. There are many stuffings suited to diverse cooking methods and regional preferences. However, I think the Quo-tik (Pan-stickers) are the best and most popular or the king would not have rewarded the sisters Fong and Yuen.

Dough:

It might surprise you that only cold water is added to the flour. You need about 2 cups of flour to 1 cup of cold water. Notice that I have already mentioned twice, "COLD". Put the flour into a large mixing bowl, add water and mix with a pair of chopsticks or a wooden mixing spoon. Set the dough aside for 5 minutes. Now use your hands to knead until soft and manageable. You can still add some dry flour during the kneading to keep your hands from sticking to the dough. Leave the dough covered for another 10 minutes.

Shaping:

First cut off a fist-size piece of dough and knead on a lightly-floured board with your hands. Form it into a broomstick shape by holding the dough up in the air and letting it drop from your hands, while your fingers are pressing, pinching and squeezing. When it is broomstick shape, place on the board and roll it with your palms into a neater shape like that of a round rod. Cut with a blunt knife into pieces the same length as the width. Sprinkle with flour and gently press with the heel of your hand, lightly rolling between the palm and the board. This will form them into balls. Flatten each ball into a circle with the heel of the palm. Roll the circle thinner with a rolling pin, **almost** to the center. This means you have to turn the circle around during the rolling and **never** let the rolling pin reach the center.

Done correctly, you will have a circle of dough for wrapping which has a thinner edge than the center. Why? For it helps you to form the dumplings later on. It sounds tricky—but it is not. Since the edge does not have to be uniform, an approximate circle is all right. If you are making the pan-stickers by yourself, you cannot expect to make too many. It will be much more fun and easier too, if another person can do the filling and forming of the dumplings while you are rolling.

Forming:

It is easy to follow the drawings, so study them, step by step.

Remarks: It will be easy for beginners to shape and form while the empty wrapping is resting on the table. Don't over-fill them. Pinch the edges together firmly or the juices will run out of the filling, make the dough soggy, and create a problem when cooking them.

Cooking:

Since the automatic electric cooker or skillet is in common usage, I will give directions for this easier method first. Set the heat control dial at 250 degrees F. or 120 degrees C. and wait until the light blinks off. Use only one tablespoon of oil in the skillet. Then place the pan-stickers neatly in rows, leaving about 1/8" space between them. A normal size cooker or skillet will hold about 30 pan-stickers which is about right for three servings.

Mix 1/3 cup water with 1 teaspoon vinegar (any kind), add to pan and cover. Switch the dial to 350 degrees F. or 180 degrees C. Wait until the indicator light goes off. The bottoms of the pan-stickers should be nicely browned. If they are over-done or under-done, the chances are your dial was not precisely set. You can easily adjust the recommended setting by increasing or decreasing the degrees of heat. Then remember this adjusted temperature setting for preparing the next batch. Serve with the bottoms up. Why? It keeps the crust crisp. Serve with light soy sauce and vinegar to personal taste.

Alternate Method:

Cook on top of the range. This is also simple. Just follow the directions for using the electric cooker. The only thing you have to judge is when the crust is nicely brown. This is not so difficult. Old-time cooks used to insist that they were the only ones who could determine when the crusts were ready. You only have to listen to the sizzling sound during cooking. When the sound lessens and then is quiet, it indicates the moisture has evaporated and the crust has started to brown. Then you lower the heat. After awhile, lift the lid and examine one of the pan-stickers. If it is not ready, cook it a little longer.

Stuffing:

The quantity of stuffing required can be easily judged by comparing the volume of dough to the stuffing prepared. You will need about one part dough to one part of the stuffing in volume.

Stuffing Recipe:
  1 lb. ground beef or pork butt
  3 T. soy sauce
  1 t. sugar
  1/2 t. pepper powder
  1 cup of chopped vegetables: Different vegetables can be used.
    I have listed them in order of personal preference.
    Chinese Cabbage (Napa Cabbage)—Medium squeezing,
    1 T. oil per cup
    Chinese Pak Choy—the same as above
    Spinach or Watercress (trimmed from tough roots)—
    Light squeezing, 1 T. oil per cup
    Onions—No squeezing, salt only
    Ordinary Cabbage—Finely chopped, heavy squeezing,
    1 T. oil per cup

All the vegetables should be chopped and salt should be added. The amount of salt to be added can easily be determined simply by digging your finger in the squeezing and tasting it. It should be more salty than usual. Why? The dough wrappings are not seasoned. Oil and squeeze them according to the side notes. Keep the natural juice in with the meat portion. Mix the meat and vegetables together to complete the stuffing.

EGG FLOWER SOUP

    4 cups of chicken broth
    1 T. of soy sauce
    1 t. of salt
    1 pinch of pepper
    2 roughly beaten eggs

Bring the broth and seasoning to a boil, add in the beaten eggs, and gently stir to prevent the eggs forming a big lump.

Remarks:

When adding the eggs, the heat should be off, the pouring of eggs should be rather slow and in small amount circling the surface of soup. Let it set for one minute without heat as this will help to cook the eggs to the right point. Garnish with 1 t. of sesame oil before serving. Chopped green onion may be added also.

THICKENED EGG FLOWER SOUP

The same as above. When the broth comes to a boil, add in 2 T. of cornstarch mixed with 6 T. of water, or thicken to the desired consistency.

Remarks:

A small amount of soy sauce or salt should be used to compensate for the extra amount of cornstarch and water. You should thicken the soup first, then add in the beaten eggs as in the last mentioned method.

FLUFFY EGG SOUP

    2 beaten eggs
    1 stalk of chopped green onions
    1 pinch of salt
    4 cups of chicken broth seasoned with salt and pepper to taste
    1 T. of oil

Heat a pot, add in the oil, cook the beaten eggs. When it is 3/4 done, pour in the seasoned broth and serve.

Remarks:

The broth should be warmed but not boiling. The egg should never be overcooked.

COLD SOUP OF MUNG BEAN THREADS AND FRIED BEAN CURD

This is a popular soup that in Eastern China is served cold in hot summer. Comparing this recipe with other westerners' Cold Soups, I feel that the Chinese ingredients are well selected. Chinese never use milk, cream, potatoes or any meat. A Cold Beef Consomme which is called Beef Tea by Chinese is not classified as a soup.

4 cups of water
1 T. of soy sauce
1 t. of salt
1/4 t. of sugar
1 cup of pre-soaked mung bean threads cut into inch long.
1 cake of bean curd, firmer type, cut it into small cubes, deep-fried until golden brown. Rinse them in hot water to get rid of excessive oil.
4 pre-soaked mushrooms, cut into slices.

Put all the above in a pot, bring to a boil, simmer for 5 minutes. Let it cool down, or chill it somehow if the weather is really hot.

Remarks:

Add in few drops of sesame oil, and hot chili oil just before serving. Chili oil can be made by cooking fresh chopped chili peppers in enough oil with very little salt, till the oil turns reddish color. Use low heat during the cooking. This can be kept very well for a long time in a cold dark place. The oil is used for garnishing and the cooked chili peppers are still usable for spicy dish, such as Curry or Hot Spice Fish.

The Eight Fairies

In China, no boy was told a bedtime story. Boys were taught to read at a desk and to sleep in bed. Perhaps for this reason, I do not read in bed and I write at a desk—although I do prefer to sleep at a desk and read in bed!

As a young boy, I was always a listener while the taletellers might be housemaids, the cook, visiting relatives or guests. Tale-telling time often occurred after din-

ner during the hot summer months. In many
parts of China, it would be too hot to sleep,
so everyone relaxed in the yard, preferably
under a tree. As the sky gradually darkened
and the stars began to twinkle, someone
always said, "What about some tales?"

Among the popular tales were those about
the Eight Fairies, each having some outstanding magic of his own. Of the eight, the most
tales were told about the Cripple Lee. Legend
said that Lee was a handsome young man—
not the shabby crippled beggar that you see in
the picture. At the time of our tale, he was
studying the miracles of fairies.

One day he told his disciples that his soul
would leave his body to roam the world for
49 days. He told them that his soul might fail
to return and re-enter his body should he fail
to achieve his goal of performing miracles. If
his soul had not returned, they were to bury
his body on the 50th day. Unfortunately, his
disciples made an error in counting the days!
When Lee's soul returned to re-enter his
body—the body had already been buried.

Lee was in a helpless situation, for his soul had to re-enter a body within limited days or his soul would gradually fade away. Therefore, only by finding a body from which a soul had recently departed, and which had not yet been buried, could he have a form to re-enter and thereby keep his soul from fading away. He found such a form in the newly deceased crippled beggar. So—this is the form he takes now, although he has the soul of a handsome young man!

THE FAIRY DUCK

By legend a fairy can do many unusual things. For him to squeeze through a key-hole is nothing. To expand himself into a giant is "duck soup," especially for this duck, so this is a Fairy Duck.

BONING METHOD:

This dish is a very classic dish. Only the original method to debone the duck has been modified to a simpler way. I was really lucky that in my boyhood I had many times seen Old Tim, our family cook, prepare it with the skill of a surgeon. He used to dress the duck himself, as the dressed duck came with the cavity already opened. After he removed the feathers, he made a slit under one wing only. This slit was cut under the "armpit." He managed to work his fingers in and loosen the internal organs. He broke the neck without breaking the skin and pulled the neck bone out through the opening, leaving only the skin of the neck. The most difficult part was the wings as he had to remove all the bones except the wing tips.

The drumsticks were broken too and only the last inch was left with the feet intact. A duck has very soft breast bones so the meat could be left inside but the bones were entirely out. Any meat attached to the bones would be removed and used in the stuffing. The purpose of this time-consuming job is to prepare the duck without any openings except the slit under the wing which would be concealed by stitching. When the duck was cooked and served it puzzled even the most cunning diner how Old Tim could prepare such a dish. Since humble Old Tim never thought to impress anyone by using his own name, he credited it to the duck, as a Fairy Duck.

This method is really too difficult and I confess that I can hardly do it. However, if an ordinary dressed duck is used, I can manage in about half an hour. With a large duck I can prepare it in even less time. I use a pair of

Chinese cooking scissors which have a sharp point but short blades which gives them better leverage. Use a chopping knife to break the neck bone and the drumsticks. I also use a small kitchen knife to loosen the meat from the cavity. The main bones of the body are not difficult to remove. Be careful not to over debone in the back which is very delicate and can be easily broken. Once they are out you twist the joints of the thighs, drumsticks, and wings. Work with a small knife and scissors to clear the meat to get out the bones. Chop at least one inch from the drumsticks and leave the wing tips too. The neck is very simple since most dressed ducks come with a slit near the head. You just break it by twisting and loosening with scissors. Work the neck skin as putting on hose or straightening a long glove. You can pull it out through the inside of the body cavity.

If you have decided not to try such a painstaking job, let me tell you that it really pays to do it. The boneless duck is like an empty elastic bag which will allow you to put in over twice the amount of stuffing as the conventional westerners' method. Afterwards the duck will look huge and just great. Because of so much stuffing, only one duck can serve up to twenty people. I know that westerners don't like the duck head to be served. In fact it is only in Chinatown that you can find a dressed duck with even a neck. The advantage in having the head and neck is that you have more space for stuffing and the duck looks more like a whole duck. If the duck is without a head you should omit the neck as it would look awful.

After the duck is completely boned, allow about 1 T. of soy sauce per net weight of one pound of boneless duck meat. Rub the duck inside with 1 T. of cooking wine and soy sauce. Use only enough soy sauce to rub the duck skin for better color.

Old Tim's cooking method cared for nothing but quality. I think most family cooks could not afford his professional touch. His stuffed duck should go for an oil-showering operation. The duck was kept in a large strainer while hot oil was poured all over it again and again until it was crispy and golden brown. I modified this tedious operation into brushing with oil and browning in the oven by broiling. I have had several miserable experiences where the duck burst so I would like to remind readers not to overstuff the duck. Also remember to soak the stuffing very well ahead of time or even overnight. This cuts the swelling during the cooking.

COOKING METHOD:

Steaming is the most appropriate method for this dish. The browning of the skin adds a pleasing color and makes it fluffy, yet firm enough to hold the expanding stuffing during the required cooking time. Medium heat gives a better penetration and is less likely to cause the duck to burst. During the steaming, moisture from the stuffing should be sufficient for the expanding ingredients. However, you may add some water, wine, or broth.

An average size duck will take at least 1 1/2 hours to steam. If you have a large steamer, I presume that you know how to use it. For those of you who do not have a proper steamer, here is a method using a Dutch oven. Put one inch of water in the Dutch oven and place a supporter, say a saucer about one inch high, in the bottom. On this supporter, use an ovenproof vessel or dish large and deep enough to catch the drippings during the steaming. Place the duck on this vessel breast-side up. When the water starts to boil, lower the heat to just a little more than simmering. Check about every 30 minutes to replace the water that has evaporated. During steaming, the duck tends to lose its nice brown color, so, just prior to adding the sauce, place the duck under the broiler for desired brownness, being careful not to burn the meat.

Place the duck on a platter. Strain all drippings, add two cups of broth or more, and thicken with cornstarch until it has the consistency of creamed soup. Season to taste, garnish with a few drops of sesame oil, and pour over the duck. Serve. Since the duck is boneless and tender, use a serving spoon to serve both meat and stuffing. Add some thickened sauce to each serving.

INGREDIENTS FOR STUFFING:

Giblets of the duck, which usually come with the duck, cut into pea-size. (Chicken giblets may also be used.) **Meat** from the removed bones should be trimmed and cut into pea-size. Ham should also be included. Chinese ham, though expensive and difficult to obtain, is my first choice, Virginia and Italian ham is second. For a third choice, you may use a thick slice of cooked ham, diced. The use of **fresh pork** smooths the other starchy ingredients. Two slices of pork chops which has lean meat interlaced with fat, cooked and diced, will suffice. **Mung Beans** should be presoaked until the hulls are loosened. This item is optional. You may substitute barley or green peas, but the barley should be well-soaked and drained. Dark dried **Chinese Mushrooms** are the best, but you may use canned or fresh mushrooms. **Bamboo shoots** are usually obtainable in cans only and should be drained and diced.

This classical dish is named the Fairy Duck with Eight Treasures. There is no set rule saying you must use precisely eight ingredients. However, I like to use eight in keeping with the legend of the Eight Fairies.

If you do not use the neck, then you will have some neck skin which should be diced and mixed with the stuffing. The bones should be used to make a broth in the correct amount of water for making sauce used in the last stage, just prior to serving. Remember to cut all ingredients into pea-size.

PROPORTION OF EACH INGREDIENT FOR STUFFING

Giblets can be added with an extra batch of chicken giblets. If your duck comes without giblets, use two batches of chicken giblets. One slice of **cooked ham steak** is more than enough. You may need only 3/4 of the slice. Use two average size **pork chops.** Do not buy the center cut. **Mushrooms** should be presoaked and should be about 1/3 of the total volume of the four parts (giblets, ham, pork, and mushrooms). Now you need twice the volume for the rest of the ingredients, which should be divided roughly into equal parts.

For those of you who like water chestnuts in a Chinese dish, this is a welcome addition. For other variations, you may use hard-boiled egg whites, diced. Beat the boiled egg yolk with raw egg and cook until well scrambled. Chop and mix into the stuffing. If the stuffing is insufficient, you may add hard-boiled and scrambled eggs instead of purchasing more ingredients and pre-soaking, both of which are time-consuming.

I sincerely hope that you will enjoy this dish which was greatly influenced by our family cook, Old Tim. He was a classically-trained chef, yet he used many unconventional methods. Many years ago, canned foods and a refrigerator were not in every home. Old Tim not only mastered established gourmet dishes, but created them through his originality, versatility and adaptability. He was not the best, but he was the greatest cook I have ever known.

FINGER GUESSING GAME

When attending a wedding ceremony dinner party, people in almost all Chinese provinces, although in different dialects, say: "I am going to drink," or "I am going to *eat* (Shanghainese) happy wine." It is obvious that the wine is more important than the food in such a celebration. The old fashioned wedding party was a very noisy one. The host and hostess, generally the mother and father of the groom, would be very satisfied if everyone made a lot of noise during the dinner party. Therefore, a game was born—"Finger Guessing." It is a very simple game in rules, yet it takes a lot of experience to master this game. Two players show a certain number of fingers at the same time, accompanied with the shout of a number which they believe will be the total of all the fingers shown by both the players. They keep on trying until one hits the correct number, then the other is the loser. There are 11 possibilities of numbers, from zero to ten. As the Chinese like to use lucky words for any occasion, each number in the game will be shouted with a fancy touch commonly used as below:

Zero   A closed fist means zero, and when one player hits the guessing number of zero, it must be to closed fists at the same time. Two does not sound very nice to Chinese, so we established a commonly used phrase—"PAIR OF TREASURE."

One   The established phrase for this number is rather difficult to be translated, because it involved some grammatical problems. What about "HOLE IN ONE?"

Two   The Chinese literary meaning is BOTH YOU AND I ARE FRIEND-LY RELATED. To adopt in into English you can say: "YOU AND ME."

Three   The popular Three Blessing Stars is used for this number. You can say "THREE STARS."

Four   Business is part of men's life, and in business we face good seasons and bad too. Therefore, it was a good wish to hope for us to have prosperity in all the four seasons. In English, I translated it as "FOUR HAPPY SEASONS."

Five   During the old time, the government staff selection was based on national public examination. There would be one first place, followed by the next four highest scores. The total would be five, and this made a phrase to wish you were the "HEAD AMONG THE FIVES."

Six   I am stuck with this phrase. It was similar to the sound of Six related to Happy in Chinese pronunciation, or with some other subtle meaning which I don't know. The well used phrase for six is (?) "HAPPY LEEWIND."

Seven   In legend the 7th of July was the date that the Weaving goddess went to meet her lover. Since July is the seventh month in the year, it was considered a coincidence. I presume it must be seven o'clock in the evening, as I don't think that they were morning joggers! Then, you can say "SEVEN-SEVEN-SEVEN!"

Eight   This is related in eastern China as Eight-fairies or in the northern China as Eight Horses, which was once a national treasure painted by a famous artist. Being a respectful artist in China will always be remembered even compared with fairies.

Nine   Owing to its pronunciation which is the same as the Chinese word of Everlasting, this phrase turns out as "EVERLASTING LONG!" Obviously it was a wish for something worthy to be everlasting long. Unluckily it was not clearly defined, therefore, what I am seeing now everlasting long in this world, are countless problems!

Ten   This is the biggest number men could count with fingers, and bigger numbers of members in a family meant richness in the ancient time. Therefore, the expression for ten is "HOME SWEET HOME." You might agree, however, to have so many dependents in your family, will be a good sum deductable.

The Magic Pillow

In the Tang Dynasty, 719 A.D., there was a Taoist named Wu. He was referred to as "Wu, the old man who knows the mystery of Tao." One day he was on his way to the capital and stopped at an inn. Soon after his arrival, a young man wearing shabby clothes and riding a skinny donkey stopped at the same inn. The two men exchanged compliments and chatted. After a while, the young man looked at his own shabby clothes and the skinny donkey and said, "What a man I am! Living without a single achievement and see how I look!"

Wu, the old man, smiled and responded "How do you look? you look well and healthy. We are chatting pleasantly. What is the matter? Why do you suddenly sigh and give me such a melancholy look?" The young man answered "I feel that I am living meaninglessly. I am a man, an educated man. I should be sent into the field as a general or to the court to serve the King as a minister. My mouth should be fed with the best of delicacies. My ears should be given the most joyful music. My eyes should be used to watch my family growing and growing. Then I could consider myself a man."

During their conversation, the innkeeper had been preparing congee, a kind of gruel made of rice—or wild rice, as was the case in this original story. Wu, the old man, said "If that is what you want, let me give you a chance to satisfy yourself. Here is a magic pillow. It will grant you your wishes."

The young man saw that it was a very strangely shaped pillow. He decided to try it, as he could not be any worse off than he was now. As soon as he placed his head on the magic pillow he felt it becoming hollower and hollower—and growing even more hollow until there was a big hole, as large as a door. The young man walked through and found himself in his native village. There he was met by the richest family in town and was asked to marry the rich man's youngest daughter—a beautiful girl!

With such a wealthy father-in-law, the young man was soon living in luxury. He was very happy. Not only did he have finely tailored suits, but carriages at his disposal. He had time to study and passed the qualification tests as a staff member of the state. He received promotion after promotion and was elevated many ranks, higher and higher. Eventually he was appointed to Commander-in-chief and finally defeated the invaders. He became one of the most important persons in the Court.

However, there were men more powerful than he in the Court and, because of the jealousy of others, he was demoted and demoted in rank. Falsely accused of plotting with the enemy to start a revolution, he was arrested and condemned to death; but due to the intervention of a person of very high rank in the Court , he was saved from execution and was exiled to a remote part of the country. After several years in exile, he was recalled to

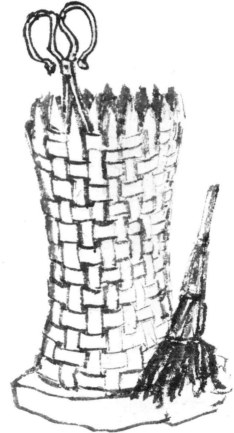

Court and given an even higher post than he had ever held before his exile.

He married and was blessed with five sons, all of whom became influential officers, serving the king. In due time, he had ten grandsons and granddaughters.

History repeated itself and twice again he was removed from his post and exiled. Yet twice he was reinstated and each time to an even more exalted position. He then served politically for fifty years and, during that time, attained the highest achievement. He had only one wife, but eight mistresses of rare beauty. He had been born in a small village, but the king gave him ten thousand acres of land and many honorable titles. Eventually, when he became old and weak, he wanted to resign, but permission was not granted. He then became very ill and was slowly dying . . . dying . . . dying . . .

At this instant, the young man suddenly awakened from his dream. He looked around and found himself still at the inn. The young man said "Was I in a dream?"

"Were you? We all were, and are still dreaming," said the venerable Wu, who was sitting beside him, smiling.

Alas, the congee was still not ready to be served because it takes a longer time—as compared to a dream!

CONGEE

Congee is a very old English word. Most recent editions of dictionaries do not include this word. The definition for congee, however, was "rice gruel" and is called "canja" in Portuguese. It is a very healthy food for breakfast. Congee supplies enough water and is one of the fast energy-

releasing agents that we need in the morning, a practice which the Chinese have used for centuries.

In our tale of "The Magic Pillow," you should have noted that the congee was mentioned in the middle section and also at the end of the tale. Since it requires more than an hour to prepare congee, this is to show the contrast that, while napping, a man had dreamed of a long life, shorter than the time for congee to be done. Therefore, this dish is never prepared in the morning for breakfast, but is prepared the previous evening. Many Chinese like to have a late snack. They prepare this type of congee which is rather light, but filling, keeping your calories before bedtime to a minimum.

To re-heat congee, put one finger of cold water in a pan, bring to a boil, and add the cold congee, but do not stir. This is an excellent method for re-heating such thickened foods as cream soups or stews to keep from burning them on the bottom of the pan.

There are many variations of congee. I selected this one to please the general taste. Since I always want even your first trial to be successful, let me suggest that you use one whole chicken leg (drumstick and thigh) for every three servings. Allow 1/4 cup of rice per three servings. Bring six cups of water to a boil and add the unwashed rice and chicken. Boil for one minute.

Cover and turn down to simmer and maintain at low heat for 1 1/2 hours. The chicken will then be very tender and the bones can be removed easily. Use two forks to divide the meat into pieces. Salt to taste and add a pinch of pepper. Serve in a bowl.

If you like such a snack, you may wish to try some other variations. The water and rice should always be simmered for at least 1 1/2 hours. Duck, ham, pork, beef and other meats will provide variations. In some parts of China, left-over rice is used, in which case just add some water and cook for five minutes. Congee is recommended for weight-watchers, as the total intake of calories is very low.

A congee-vendor in San Francisco has a scroll hanging on the wall with brush calligraphy of an old famous poem with the title of "Congee." It is quite interesting that the composer made the congee into a philosophy in poetry. I hope I can remember it and share its original expression with you.

"Chatting with my wife in time free,
A rare case that we both do agree.
With the same amount of rice,
One meal stretches by twice.
When friends come unexpectedly,
Just add more water accordingly.
Don't you ever complain
The taste is bland and unexciting.
Remember, my dear friend,
Blandness is a taste everlasting.

It is remarkable how the Chinese can always find so much interesting philosophy—even in such a simple everyday thing as Congee.

CONGEE VARIATIONS:

Various combinations can be used with congee by the quick-boiling method.

BEEF CONGEE

4 cups of basic congee, seasoned to taste with salt
4 oz. of beef, sliced, mixed with 2 t. of oil.

Keep congee at boiling point, add beef slices,
stir gently, and turn off the heat.
Wait for 2 minutes and serve.

FISH CONGEE

4 cups of basic congee
4 oz. of fillet of fish, thinly sliced
    (preferably fresh water fish)
2 t. of oil to be mixed with
    the fish slices

Since fish is very easy to cook, especially in such thin slices, you only have to heat the congee to a boil. Fill individual bowls with congee and add in the fish slices at the table when serving. Garnish with chopped green onion and ginger.

PORK AND PRESERVED EGGS CONGEE

4 oz. of salt pork, cut into small pieces
1 perserved egg (also called the Thousand Years Egg) shelled and halved.
1/2 cup of rice
6 cups of water

This is a very intelligently created dish, as the alkalai content in the preserved egg turns the congee into a pleasing flavor and a different kind of smooth texture. Simmer at low heat for an hour, breaking the eggs into small pieces before serving.

FRESH EGGS USED IN CONGEE

For adding quantity or quality, eggs can be added to congee at anytime. Beat the eggs, add in slowly when congee reaches a boil. Turn the heat off, allow to set for 10 seconds, stirring very gently so the eggs will not form into a ball. Allow to set for another few minutes before serving.

CHOPPED LETTUCE USED IN CONGEE

Chopped lettuce gives a special crunchiness to the congee and the addition should be made just before serving. The quantity of lettuce should be about 1/8 of the total volume of congee.

The Boatman's Dish

During the Ming Dynasty, four of the best scholars passed a national examination and became famous for their culture. The national examination was the traditional method of selecting staff members for the government. This tradition ended when Chinese Nationalism was born in 1911. The four famous scholars were named Tong, Chuk, Wen, and Chou. Tong was a well-known brush painter and a very romantic man. Chuk was shortsighted, old and ugly, but very highly skilled in calligraphy and very witty. Wen was a serious scholar and Chou was very handsome. They had entered for the same examination and so became friends.

There are hundreds of legends and tales about these four men. There were tale-tellers who earned their living by telling only parts of these legends. Believe it or not—some subtle tale-tellers could manage to hold your interest for days without reaching the end of the story. For example, one story is about a young girl in her boudoir dressing and putting on her make-up—readying herself to go downstairs and meet her beau. The tale-teller did not need a staircase of a million steps; instead, he described what the girl was

doing and what she was feeling. That was enough! He ended the daily two-hour session by saying, "Tomorrow, let us see what will happen when the girl meets her beau." The next day, he ended with the same words because he had improvised so much that when the two hours had passed, the girl was still in her boudoir! It sounds as if he were cheating, but the listeners never complained because, each day, the tale-teller held their undivided attention for those two hours. One famous tale-teller kept the girl in her boudoir for exactly one week! Maybe only Scheherazade could have equaled this feat!

The tale of "The Boatman's Dish" was recorded in a book. Its author actually collected hundreds of stories told by many people. He edited them into a book of four volumes and it is a most enjoyable book to read. Part of the story was told like this:

Tong, the brush painter, was visiting a temple. He saw a young girl kneeling in front of a god, silently praying for a blessing. Captivated by her fascinating beauty, Tong approached her and knelt by her side. To catch her attention he murmured jokingly, "My merciful God, please help me to marry as beautiful a girl as this one at my side. I promise to love her and if I am not true to her, let me drown in FIRE and burn in WATER." The girl heard the naughty man at her side, and she could not help but giggle at his

jestful praying. Well, this smile completely enchanted Tong and he decided to follow her. The girl, who was from a rich family, left the temple in a carriage and boarded a large junk for a long trip up the river. Tong, who had no carriage and therefore had great difficulty trying to follow on foot, arrived minutes too late at the wharf and disappointedly watched the junk departing!

He asked the only nearby boatman to take him on a trip to chase the junk. After some bargaining, the boatman agreed to do so. It wasn't a very pleasant voyage in such a small, shabby boat—but subtle tale-tellers can keep you listening to the tale for days and it can still be a long, long time before the small boat catches up with the junk. Maybe tomorrow, when the wind changes, the small boat might catch up with the junk. Who can tell? This author does not plan to keep you, reader, too long, so let us come to the part of the story which relates to this book . . .

It was dinnertime and the boatman started to eat his rice. Tong was also very hungry but couldn't complain because he had asked the boatman to chase the junk and time had not allowed the boatman to arrange for a pleasure trip with a delicious meal. Tong, who was accustomed to good food, could hardly eat a single grain of plain salted rice, which was all that was available.

"Aren't you going to eat your rice, sir?" asked the boatman.

"I have never had just plain rice," replied Tong.

"Well, it isn't my fault since you didn't even allow me to buy some food. Now it is too late, so why don't you try to help yourself by thinking of something pleasant which might give you greater appetite," said the boatman, wisely.

"How would that be possible, you stupid boatman," said the now angry (as well as hungry!) Tong.

"Aha," the boatman retorted. "I also don't like to eat my rice without a single tasty dish. But I keep thinking that since you promised to pay me a double fee, I can plan to use the money to repair my fishing gear. Then I will catch more fish and more fish will bring me more money. With more money, I will eventually find a girl to marry me. So with those happy thoughts, my mouth waters, I am eating well and I am content with what I have."

"Oh, no!" said Tong. "This could not apply to me."

"Well," responded the boatman, "Let me help you. You hold your bowl with your left hand and your chopsticks with your right hand. Look at your rice and be ready to eat. I will call out a full banquet by naming the courses. As I say each name, you must recall the taste of that dish. Then you will feel a longing for that dish and your mouth will certainly water. Now, before it dries up, quickly help yourself to a mouthful of rice. Ready?"

Tong was tempted.

"Now," the boatman went on, "this course is 'Shelled Fresh Water Shrimp' tenderly cooked and garnished with lemon juice."

Tong, who was a shrimp fancier, recalled such a delightful dish, and the aroma of lemon juice blended so nicely with the shrimp that his mouth watered and he ate a mouthful of rice! The boatman was illiterate but that did not mean that he wasn't wise. He must also have been a very imaginative gourmet or he couldn't have enticed Tong to finish a bowlful of rice without any accompaniment but salt.

The first recorded dish was really a shrimp dish. Now allow me to explain that this dish was shrimp only, without any complements. Because complements such as bamboo shoots, onions, etc., were usually much cheaper, to have a dish of nothing but shrimp took twice as much shrimp—thus it was considered an elegant, delicate gourmet dish. I couldn't find a name for this dish that would express the name in the simple Chinese way. I was in despair, then suddenly I thought, this is a dish with nothing but shrimp; why don't I call it "Nothing but Shrimp?" I have served it many times and it has proven a welcome dish. The name is simple, yet tells the truth.

The mention in the foregoing story of shrimp being garnished with lemon juice was simply for better understanding by my readers. Actually, Chinese never use lemons in cooking—we use vinegar. However, if I had named vinegar as the garnish, you might have been confused. This word of explanation may assist my readers to share the appetizing effect of vinegar.

NOTHING BUT SHRIMP

Freshwater shrimp is used for this established dish as they can be purchased jumpingly alive in many parts of China. This dish is considered difficult to prepare as the shrimp must be crunchy. I tried many different methods, got hints from many chefs, but none of them could tell me the point that determined success or failure. Then I discovered that the secret is to soak-dry the shrimp. Even though you may also know this, I doubt whether you do it my way.

First decide on the quantity of shrimp needed. Shrimp are classified in

numbers per pound. I prefer the 25/30 pieces per pound. Never buy the small size which not only is more work to shell, but also renders less meat per pound. To shell the shrimp is easy. Just flip its underneath opening with the thumb. The tail part can easily be shelled by pulling lightly with the fingers of one hand squeezing (as you squeeze the end of a tube of toothpaste) with the fingers of the other. Slit the back so you can trim out the veins. First, shell the shrimp, then cut slits, devein, and then wash them.

To wash, use 1 teaspoon of baking soda per pound of shrimp (gross weight). Mix well, let stand for ten minutes, and wash them in cold running water for several minutes. Drain well. You may put the shrimp in a strainer, set inside a bowl, and leave overnight in the refrigerator. The shrimp should be covered with a piece of paper towel. This will make the next step much easier.

To soak-dry, use good quality paper towels. One sheet is just right for a pound of shelled shrimp. Place the shrimp neatly in rows. Place another sheet of paper towel on top, press firmly and gently with both hands, fingers widespread. Now, this is my proven method. Turn over the moistened two sheets of paper towel. Remove the sheet that is now on top and discard. Place a fresh sheet on top and repeat the pressing and turning over. Do this again and again until the towel is only slightly moist. This means the shrimp are dry enough, since no excess moisture comes out, even by pressing. Unless the shrimp are drained overnight, you will need about six to seven sheets of paper towels to reach this stage.

Now the shrimp are ready for the marinade, which is given below:

    1 egg white
    1 t. of cornstarch
    1 t. of salt
    1/2 t. of sugar
    Pinch of white pepper
    1 t. of oil

Add the shelled shrimp and mix well. This can be done hours in advance. I used to add wine to almost any kind of marinade, but this was corrected by my elder sister. I fully agree with her now since I have already found the secret in shrimp was dryness. Wine is required, but later when the shrimp have been cooked. Because the shrimp have been cooked, the wine will not penetrate, making them soggy, but gives a nice aroma. If you have followed instructions faithfully up to now, the rest is very simple. (I searched for possible effects of the temperature of the oil before discovering that dryness was the solution!)

Now simply heat the cookware normally. If you are using a wok, you need about 3 tablespoons of oil for one pound of shrimp; but only 2 tablespoons for Teflon-coated ware. Put in one slice of ginger root and the white part of one stalk of green onion to season the oil first. Place the marinated shrimp into a wok or skillet. Use a cooking spoon to separate them quickly, and keep turning and separating them so the shrimp can be evenly cooked by the heated oil. After a minute or so, depending on your heat, the shrimp are almost done. Add a few drops of wine which will evaporate in seconds. Add a few drops more and the steam created will shorten the cooking time. When the shrimp are firm, it is almost time to serve. Season to taste. Add several drops of sesame oil, one more pinch of pepper, and 1 teaspoon of Chinese red vinegar. Umm! This is simply delicious! (Use red wine vinegar, never the garlic-seasoned type as it gives an unpleasant odor.) Before serving, remove the browned ginger and onion.

I hope that you, reader, will understand well about the preparation of shrimp for any other shrimp dish. The given method of drying by soaking is invaluable for success in other shrimp dishes. Suggested combinations will then be simple to follow.

SHRIMP WITH EGGS

1 lb. shelled shrimp (weight is *with* shells and this will be enough for 4 servings.)
4 eggs, roughly beaten
1 t. salt
Pinch of powdered pepper
1 t. of dry white table wine
1 egg-size of water (measure with two halves of a broken shell)
1 t. of cornstarch

Use 2 T. of oil to cook the shrimp, adding wine to produce more steam which will help the cooking. When the shrimp are done, put them in the bowl of beaten eggs with seasoning. Using a clean wok or skillet, very hot, add 3 T. oil and pour in the batch of shrimp and eggs, beating the batch before pouring as the cornstarch is likely to settle to the bottom of the bowl. Do not stir the eggs as if you were scrambling them. With a cooking spoon, push them from one side to another, making the uncooked portion get into the center, where the heat is higher. Repeat this procedure until all eggs are set and done.

Here are some helpful hints to make this dish successful:

1. More oil might be needed during the cooking of the eggs, and should be sparingly added around the edges.
2. One teaspoon of wine can be added just before serving to give a pleasing aroma.
3. A rarely known professional touch is to add exactly 1 t. of red vinegar just before serving. You will be amazed how it changes the flavor of this dish! Cooking is an art and Chinese have studied it for thousands of years.

Follow the cooking method for Chinese-fried Eggs. Of course use the ingredients called for in this dish.

FANCY TERMS

Once a man was giving a party and had invited many of the guests to stay overnight at his house. He had two servants of whom the older one was intelligent, but the younger one was not so bright. During the party, the younger noticed that the host always said, "Please, please," when a dish was placed on the table. This puzzled the young servant boy. He asked the older servant why the host did not say "Eat, eat." The older one explained, "It is very rude to say, "Eat, eat." It is more polite, elegant, and better manners to say "Please," which means to eat."

When clearing the tables, the younger one found that the chopsticks were not made of wood as he thought they should be, but of something like bone. He asked the older one if these were made of a special kind of bone. The older one smiled and said, "How can you say they are made of bone! They are made of IVORY." This puzzled the younger one again and he now thought it was better manners to call bone "ivory." Just before the host and his guests were going to bed, the younger one heard the host say "Sweet dreams." This time the younger did not bother to ask anymore, for he was certain that when one wanted to "sleep," one should say "sweet dreams" as it was more polite.

Several days later, the younger servant got a fish bone caught in his throat. It was so serious that the could not even finish his meal and went to bed. Sharing the same quarters and hearing the restless noise, the older servant asked the younger one what was wrong. Remembering all that he had learned from the party, the younger one, trying to impress his colleague, said:

> "I am hungry as I did not 'please-please' my dinner, and the 'ivory' is hurting me so much in my throat, I can't 'sweet dreams'."

The moral of this story is never to use fancy terms without understanding them. In serving a Chinese dish, if you are not Chinese, the best way is to use plain English in describing it. On the next page, I have tried to give you the background of some commonly used terms in Chinese cooking, so you can better understand their meaning.

SOME COMMONLY USED FANCY TERMS IN CHINESE MENUS:

FU YUNG:
Egg whites are used in this dish and are added during the thickening stage, instead of using cornstarch. Egg whites give a different kind of texture and color. Fu-Yung is the Chinese name of a flower, whose English name is hibiscus. When properly applied for thickening, the cooked egg white will have an irregular form, assuming the form of petals of the flower Fu-Yung. Someone invented the dish Fu-Yung eggs, made of assorted meat and vegetables with eggs, by the method of scrambling eggs in the form of a cake. How absurd!

SUB GUM:
Trying to use English spelling for Chinese words will only confuse you. The first time an American asked me about Sub-Gum, it sounded like Sub-gun and this seemed strange in Chinese cooking. I was surprised. The better translation, although it has lost its original fanciness of meaning, is "Assorted," which means that the dish is cooked with assorted ingredients.

HUNG-TU:
This is actually the same as Sub-Gum, which means many ingredients were used in the dish. Literally, it means in Chinese "A Great Plan." Since a great plan should be great, so a dish named Hung-tu should have better quality ingredients, while Sub-gum will have more in numbers, but not necessarily fancy ingredients.

PAK-PO:
This is literally the Eight Treasures, but that does not mean that the dish has eight ingredients. It is really only because Chinese liked to play with words. Sub-gum, Hung-tu, and Eight Treasures are basically the same, but Chinese had the established custom to give each dish different names.

CHE-LIU:
This is chicken's loin cut into thin slices and nicknamed Willow-Leaves. It was supposed to use only the loins, but since each chicken has merely two small pieces of loin, (willow-leaves shape), it now includes the chicken breast. However, only the breast and the loin should be used for this dish.

YUE-SHANG:
This is the fish flavor achieved by special blending of seasoning and spices without acutally using fish. Knowing this will avoid any misunderstanding about this dish.

KWAI-WHA: This is literally the Cinnamon blossom, a tiny, round, yellowish flower. When a whole beaten egg is used for the final thickening, the cooked egg will be firm. By breaking it into tiny bits, the appearance is assumed to be like a Cinnamon blossom.

KUNG-PO: This was actually an officer's title of rank among many ancient Chinese officers. A member of that rank was noted for his family cooking and many of his recipes are still being used. So, Kung-po dishes signify that the recipes were created by a man with the title of Kung-po, but no two dishes are alike because each dish will have different types of seasoning or combinations of ingredients.

LU-HAN: This is always used for a vegetarian dish, when a variety of very expensive gourmet mushrooms are included which resemble heads of Lu-han, gods in Buddhism religion. Therefore, unless this particular kind of mushroom is used, it should not be referred to as Lu-han.

E-FU: In literal translation is Family of E, a famous rich gourmet. He created an unconventional method of serving noodles by first deep-frying the fresh noodles which had been partially cooked in water. This changes the texture and stands as a gourmet variation of a noodle dish. He applied the same principle to Won-ton, creating a new dish now known as E-Fu Won-ton, which reverses the procedure by partially deep-frying the Won-ton first, then cooking them in soup.

STRATEGY OF FINGER GUESSING

By using a loud and strong voice, you can somehow scare your opponent. If you notice that he has a favorite number that he has a habit of repeating, 3 for instance, use different fingers each time yourself, but always add 3 to it and call this number to make a hit. As soon as the 3 appears you will eventually win the game. Many times you can make a direct hit on the first try. If this happened, stick your arm high in the air with fingers as iron, motionlessly as if you were sure to hit his numbers. This will really discourage your opponent, he will make more mistakes, and you can easily beat him in following matches.

SCORING SYSTEMS

For a social party, this game is only to let guests have a simple method to break the formal mood. The loser is obliged to finish a drink. It must be rather puzzling to non-Chinese as you can hardly define whether it was a reward or penalty. However, not everybody can drink heavily so a known non-drinker was always excused, and only had to take a sip or even soft drink instead of wine. After all, a party is for having fun, not for embarrassing anyone.

For people who enjoyed challenging in this game, there is a score system as Three-in-a-row. i.e. you must win (or lose) three time consecutively. This system prevents one player with luck from winning as it often happens in the one score system.

ACROSSING THE BRIDGE

This is a system for strong players. Usually you use 5 cups in a row, fill the cups at ends only 1/4 full, the next two cups 1/2 full and the center cup full. Cups are placed in a line between two players. The loser takes the cup nearer to him, and so on. The players can still make this game more difficult if they agreed to apply the rule of Three-in-a-row for each score, or otherwise, in simple one score system, However, there will never be a draw. One of the players will reach on the bridge, or worse down the bridge, and the worst acrosses the bridge.

When the opponent is a new friend, if you win you should say, "Thanks, you let me win." If you lost, you should say, "What a good hand! Thanks for your teaching me."

Yes, Chinese are very polite people, and now let's see how intimate friends are talking before and after such a match . . .

"Hey, you rice-pot and wine-skin, dare you match with me?"

"I will beat you as easily as I take something out of my pocket!"

"It takes miles to prove a horse, and seconds to prove that you are nuts!"

"To catch you is just like catching a turtle in a jar!"

When you lost a game, you don't have to lose face. Here are what many losers will say . . .

"A gentleman never wins the first match!"

"What is wrong tonight, is the moon rising in the west?"

"I am thirsty, this is just fine for me to warm up!"

When good friends are gathered, it is lots of fun. One famous proverb goes like this, "With your intimate, a thousand cups of wine is very little, with whom you don't like, half a sentence is too much talk."

I don't know how to end this page. Maybe, let us play with wine, but don't let wine play us. It sounds really easy, as the great Mark Twain said he had no difficulty in quitting smoking, because he had done it hundreds of times!

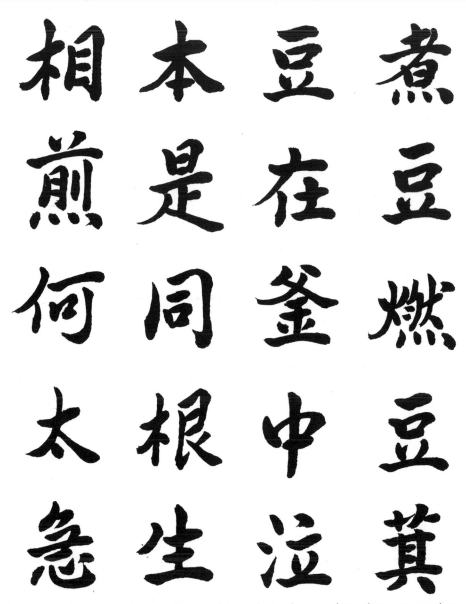

相 本 豆 煮
煎 是 在 豆
何 同 釜 燃
太 根 中 豆
急 生 泣 萁

Since this book is planned not only for cooking, but also to introduce to readers who like to know more about Chinese which has so many differences in all respect to westerners. So I fill this page with our Chinese literature, I am sure you will find it as different as Chinese cuisine is.

Chinese (classic) reads vertically from the top to bottom and from the right to the left. Chinese writing always tried to omit as many as possible of any articles, prepositions, verbs, etc; as far as the meaning is understood and fully expressed. This famous Seven Pace Poem had only twenty characters as printed above. Close and direct translation will certainly make no sense to readers. However it might be interesting for you to read the following:

Cook bean burning bean bush bean at pot inside weep
Originally were same root grown both grilling why too hurry

To make it readable to westerners, it should be:
Burning bean bush to cook the bean, Bean in the pot is weeping. Originally we were grown from the same root, Why should you punish me in such a hurry?
But, this kind of translation has lost its rhythm and simplicity. So I modified the verses which I hope readers might share my effort in keeping the expression and rhythm, and simplicity in words which is a must in a Chinese poem.

The Weeping Bean

It is recorded in history that, during the Three Kingdom period, a certain king had two sons. The elder one was very envious of his younger brother because of his learning and culture. The younger brother was respected and beloved by everyone, including his father, the king. The elder brother wanted to degrade his brother, but he could not find a good excuse. One day, they met in the kitchen where the cook was preparing a pot of beans. The fuel for the fire was dried bean bush. He said to his younger brother, "Everyone says you are a good poet. I am sorry to say that I have also heard that you bribed many people to say so! This is not honorable. I want you to prove to me that you are a good poet. I will allow you to walk slowly for

seven paces and, in the time this takes you, create a poem."

"Oh, brother," replied the younger, "I have never thought I was as gifted as you are." "Stop such nonsense and prove it to me, or I will think that you have sly intentions to demean me," angrily replied the elder brother. "Oh, I just don't know how I can convince you that I really have no such intentions at all. You are the elder one. You will be the one to take our father's post someday, when eventually and unhappily our father leaves us," responded the younger. "That is another matter. As I am the elder son, I will certainly be the successor to **my**, I mean—**our** father," said the elder, "but now I want you to prove how good you are at poetry." "But how can I compose a poem without having an inspiration?" asked the younger.

Looking around and searching for the most unsuitable subject for a poem, the elder brother said, " 'The Cooking Bean' is the title I am giving you. Don't delay! You will have seven paces to compose a sensible poem."

The poor—no! The heaven-gifted young brother started to walk because he knew it would be useless to reason with his elder brother, but let God give him inspiration. He then composed one of the greatest poems in Chinese culture, especially so when you understand the background. He calmly walked and finished the four lines that are required for a Chinese poem. The original poem consisted of only twenty words. It is impossible to translate it into English without losing its meaning or increasing the number of words as the rhythm would be completely lost. Hopefully, readers can share the feeling of this tale and this Seven-pace-poem:

> Bean is weeping in the pot,
> While bush is flaming hot.
> We came from the same family,
> Must you cook me so harshly?

BEAN SPROUT SOUP

There are two varieties of bean sprouts, although most Westerners are familiar only with the mung bean sprouts which are used for dishes such as Chop Suey or sometimes as a garnish. Soy Bean sprouts have many more uses. They make a delicious soup which can be simmered for a long time without losing their form. They can be stewed, Chinese-fried, or chopped and cooked with meat.

If you cannot purchase bean sprouts, why don't you try growing your own? This is fairly simple. Soak soy beans in water overnight, enough to cover plus two inches. Drain, put in a colander and cover with a folded kitchen towel. The colander should be kept out of the sunshine. Water the beans early in the morning, during the meal hours, and the last thing before going to bed. When watering pour cold water through the towel two or three times. Place it in the sink to drain. The sprouting will take several days. Examine the sprouts during watering. They should reach a length of about two inches and always be a shining white color.

Now to introduce you to this delicious soup. I suggest you do some home curing of meat. Allow one sparerib of pork per serving. Cut the ribs apart and crack them in the middle. Calculate the weight and use one tablespoon of salt per pound of ribs. Then add some saltpeter which can be purchased from the drugstore. The saltpeter should not exceed 10% of the amount of salt used. If you use only two pounds of ribs, you will need two tablespoons of salt—that is, six teaspoons. Ten percent of six teaspoons is approximately 1/2 teaspoon. Mix the salts together and rub the mixture all over the ribs. Leave at room temperature for several hours. If the local temperature is cooler than 40 degrees, keep them for several days outside the house in a covered metal container. If this is not possible, then keep them uncovered in the refrigerator. Turn them over every day, and in several days they will be drier. Expose them to strong sunshine during the day, if possible; if not, wrap them individually with paper towels. Again put them in a paper bag and keep the bag in the crisper of your refrigerator. One week's curing will be enough. Wash with cold tap water, and they are ready for soup. Since you are curing the meat, you should time the first mentioned method to prepare your soy bean sprouts. If you start both at the same time, normally they will be ready at the same time. Local temperatures affect the time required. After a few trials, you will know.

For a soup to serve six, you will need about a half cup of soy beans for sprouting. Put the sprouts and cured pork bones together in a pot. Fill with water, allowing two cups per serving. Bring to boil and simmer for 1 1/2 hours. The cured ribs add an excellent flavor. The sprouts will give a very clear, tasty soup with a delicate aroma. Since the ribs are heavily salted, you might not need any more salt. However, final adjustment will be required. I like the tale of "The Weeping Bean." It is one of our greatest stories. I like this soup, too—it is typically Chinese.

The Ending of the Sung Dynasty

At the end of the Sung Dynasty, the last two kings were unable to protect China from being invaded by Mongolians. The capital in the center of China was evacuated to the east. No other dynasty has ever had so many shameful pages in Chinese history as the Sung. The kings, unsuccessful in trying to keep an honorable peace, employed such means that I, a Chinese, feel ashamed to mention. The kings' mother was exchanged as ransom for a general whose army fought courageously against the Mongolians. A beautiful woman was sent on a "Diplomatic Mission" to negotiate a temporary peace! When she was about to cross the border, she left a most touching song of sadness, "Am Going." Her name was Wong Tsou-chuen.

A general, who was executed without a trial, left us a lot to be remembered. One famous saying is "If you want to condemn a person, you don't have to give reasons, or there could be a lot of reasons." The general's name was Yiu Fei. Yiu was his family name, since the family name is given first in Chinese. It means a respectful mountain. Fei means flying. According to history, his mother bore him while dreaming about a giant flying bird who found no place to pause. Yiu Fei left one short slogan for his troops, "Return us our rivers and mountains taken by the enemy." The order to execute Yiu Fei was given by Chin Kwai, the Minister-in-Chief. In Chinese, we refer to this position as "under only one man (the king), but above ten thousands (the people)."

Some modern, historical scholars defend Chin Kwai as he acted under the king's orders to execute Yiu Fei, the most beloved fighting hero. However, Chin-Kwai is referred to as the "number one traitor" in Chinese history because people were angry about the execution. In South America, people make a figure of a man and call it Judas who sold Jesus Christ. They burn the effigy of Judas in a festival in memory of Jesus Christ. Likewise, the Chinese made two pieces of dough, representing Chin Kwai and his wife, deep-fried it, and ATE it! It is perhaps one of the highest symbolic protests in history and has lasted hundreds of years. This original dough was named Fried Kwai, which sounds so uncivilized. As in the case of "Barbarian's Head," the world "Kwai" was changed into Devil—they sound similar in Chinese. Therefore, no more gruesome association to an already dead person; hence, to deep-fry a devil, which even the merciful God would approve.

Kwai, which is a spruce tree, was often used for men's names. Since this incident involving Chin Kwai, it is doubtful if there are any Chinese who use the name except those who never knew the story. In modern slang, because it is always made with two pieces of dough attached, Chinese use it to describe a couple who are always together—for better or worse.

Although the Fried Devil seems to be extremely simple in recipe form, it takes some practice and experience to make a Fried Devil of good quality. There are restaurants in San Francisco that serve Fried Devil and they serve it under different names, the worst of which is "Chinese Donut." What a ridiculous translation! None of the restaurants serve a genuine Fried Devil. One is always too oily, one is often only half-cooked, one has a strong chemical smell from using an excess amount of a special baking agent to make the dough fluffy, and still another produces Fried Devil so hard it can be used to beat rhythm on a drum.

FRIED DEVILS

There are many recipes using various methods of preparing this dish. To use sour dough is not very practical for family cooking; therefore this recipe is selected. However, you still need the determination to practice many times until you understand this kind of dough.

For the beginner with no baking or cake-making experience, this will probably not be the recipe you expected. To those who have the experience, it will be a challenge.

For 100 parts of water, dissolve the following:
  4 parts of salt
  5 parts of baking soda
  1 part of Ammonium Carbonate
  2 parts of sugar
To make a workable dough for a small batch, use:
  2 cups of water
  1 T. salt
  1 T. of baking soda
  1/4 t. of Ammonium Carbonate
  1/2 t. of sugar

If you understand the function of each ingredient, then if you have an undesirable result, you can find the problem and make the correction. Water is used for making the flour into dough; salt is the main seasoning; baking soda helps the first fermentation; Ammonium Carbonate helps the texture during the deep-frying operation. Sugar is not for sweetening but for coloring—to achieve a light golden color after frying. So, adjust the measurement by increasing or decreasing accordingly for the second trial.

The above mixture can be used as the liquid to make any amount of self-rising flour into dough, the limit is less than a pound. That is, put some flour, say 14 ounces, and add the liquid to make a dough. Mix slowly with a spoon or a pair of chopsticks. In a small quantity there will be no way to predetermine the amount of water required. When the desired texture of the dough is reached (I do hope you know what DESIRED TEXTURE means) it should be RIGHT between too soft and to hard to handle the dough. Of the afore-mentioned two cups of water, if used with 14 ounces of flour, there should be a few tablespoonsful of water left. This is a guide for you to follow.

Knead the dough very gently and let it relax. This is very important to the final result. Set the dough aside for 30 minutes, then knead it again with gentleness, let it relax again for another 30 minutes. In case the dough is too wet and soft to handle, a small amount of flour can be added.

Shaping—With your hands, shape the dough in the form of a plank, about two inches in width, and about 1/4 of an inch thick. Cut it with a knife into strips of about 1/4 x 1/4 x 2 inches. Place one strip on top of another and press it firmly with the back edge of a knife. This keeps the two strips in one piece during the frying operation.

Now hold both ends with your hands, lengthen it by a gentle pulling motion; place it in a WOK (this time, no other ordinary deep-frying pot can do the job) which has enough oil heated to 350 degrees.

During the frying, press the dough (or the devils) downward into the oil so they will be done evenly all the way through. Watch the color—when it is lightly golden brown and fluffy, it is time to remove it. Drain on paper towels and serve.

VARIATIONS TO USE THE FRIED DEVILS

Cut dough into 1/2 inch lengths. Serve with soy sauce for a dip as this is a very established way to serve it with plain congee. Cut them into 1/4 inch or less, in round slices, and add to congee which was seasoned just before serving.

The following is a dish for daily family use, simple but delightful.

8 inches of fried devils, cut into 1/8" rounds

2 eggs

3 egg-size of water or broth (use shells to measure)

1 t. of salt

2 t. of soy sauce

1 stalk of green onion, chopped

1 pinch of pepper

2 t. of oil

Mix them all together, beat the eggs, put into a shallow dish. Cook by steam at medium heat. If possible, keep the temperature at 200 degrees. Steam for 10 minutes or until firm.

If you have an electric skillet, it can serve very well as a steamer. Place a rack or a small saucer in the skillet. Fill with water until it reaches the rim of rack or saucer. Place the dish to be steamed on the support (rack or saucer), set the dial at 200 degrees. Check for doneness after 10 minutes or so.

THE THUNDERING SOUP

This dish is well known as Sizzling Soup, but I prefer the name I used as THE THUNDERING SOUP. The method of preparing and serving is my own way which will be much easier and more reliable.

Rice-biscuit:

Layer bottom of a 10-inch pie plate with a bare covering of unwashed rice. Cover rice with 1/2 inch of water. Bring to a boil, then simmer for ten minutes. Dip flat spoon into cold water, and press and smooth surface of rice to make it firm. Leave it overnight. When it is cold, bring it out, and cut the round piece into domino size.

Soup:

Use plain broth. Season to taste.

Ingredients:

1 slice of cooked ham, cut into 10 equal parts
1 piece of canned bamboo shoots, cut into slices as ham
4 medium size black mushrooms, presoaked, cut the same
1 oz. of Chinese Sze-chuen Pickles, washed, cut the same
1/2 of a skinned chicken breast, thinly sliced, marinate with
    1/2 unbeaten egg white
    1/4 t. of salt
    1/2 t. of sugar
    1/2 T. of white wine
    1T. of cornstarch
    1 t. of peanut oil

Cooking:

You should have one pot of oil, heated up to 350 degrees, ready for the rice-biscuit. Bring the chicken broth to a boil, add in the ham, bamboo shoots, mushrooms, pickles, and the chicken breast. Lower the heat for simmering ONE minute only. Take off the heat, and serve in a soup bowl, garnishing with a few drops of sesame oil. Return to the heated oil, deep-fry the cut rice-biscuit till nicely brown.

Serving:

Bring the soup bowl to the table, immediately dump the fried rice biscuit into the soup.

Remarks:

The sizzling sound is produced because the difference in temperature between the soup and fried-biscuit. Therefore, the soup should not be too hot, (that was why you made the soup first and left it aside), but the rice-biscuit must be more than 350 degrees hot.

The Dragon-Boat Festival

Tzong is the nearest possible pronunciation of the Chinese name of a food which has a long story. It looks like a tamale. In the Warring States Dynasty, 295 B.C., there was a man named Cheu Yuen, one of the high ranking officers of a king. Times were bad. He submitted many plans to the king for the improvement of living conditions of the people, but the king did not truly care about his subjects.

Cheu Yuen was a scholar. With suffering and sorrow, he wrote a famous poem to express his feeling of regretfulness, then committed suicide by drowning in the River Mi-lo, located in the Hu-nan Province. It was on the 5th of May by the Moon Calendar. This was called the Dragon-boat Festival. It was changed to the Day of the Patriotic Poet in recent years.

When Cheu Yuen attempted to commit suicide, the people who lived by the river tried to rescue him. Many of them did not know how to row a boat against the strong current of the river so they were unable to save Cheu Yuen. After futile searching, the would-be rescuers returned to the shore. The few who knew how to row a boat blamed the others for their lack of skill. Otherwise the great man might have been rescued.

The village people, even though they had failed to save Cheu Yuen's life, wanted to at least save his body from being eaten by fish. A suggestion was made that food be dumped in the river so the fish would not bother to eat the beloved man. The suggestion was well received so they made small packages of food and dumped them in the river in the area where they guessed Cheu Yuen's body might be. They beat drums and gongs in order to frighten away the big fish. The dragon was an imaginary creature which they greatly feared so they decorated their boats with the likeness of a dragon. To make certain there would be a capable rescue team available in the future, the people decided to practice rowing and have a competition on the 5th day of May in memory of this great man.

Although thousands of years have passed, the Tzong is still made and is now a favorite snack, although the original meaning is actually lost.

For many years, families exchanged Tzong as greetings during the Dragon-boat Festival.

TZONG

It seems to me that soon these old time snacks will be outmoded and nobody will have a chance to see how these fancy snacks looked. Here are pictures to give you a chance to look if they are not possible to create. There is a special kind of leaf, something like a gladiola leaf, used for Tzong by eastern Chinese. Southern Chinese use only the leaves of a giant variety of bamboo which are about a foot long, so they have to overlap them one after another to complete the wrapping.

So readers may have a chance to try the taste, if you don't insist on the shape, I can offer you the following procedure:

Soak a cup of rice overnight in cold water, drain before use. Marinate a few pieces of pork, preferably the fresh bacon type, in soy sauce—about 2 T. per 8 oz. of meat, 1 t. of sugar, and 1 T. of dry white wine.

Find some small strong wide-mouth jars which will be easy to empty after the contents are cooked.

Now, your problem may be in finding the dry bamboo leaves which are very inexpensive in Chinatown. Rinse the leaves with cold water, wash away any dirt and in minutes they will turn soft and can be cut with a pair of scissors for lining the jar. Cut two round pieces for the bottom and the top. When the jar is lined, fill 1/3 with the soaked rice, which should be seasoned with salt and soy sauce to taste. Roughly 1 T. of soy sauce per cup of soaked rice and a pinch of salt for extra saltiness; fill the second 1/3 with marinated pork, fill the last 1/3 with seasoned soaked rice. Do not pack tightly, filling should be loose. Top the jar with the round leaf you cut for it, add 1/4 jar of water, and put on the lid.

Now put the jar in a pot, fill the pot with water to cover, bring to a boil, then simmer for 2 hours. You will be amazed! Its texture is something that you never had before. Because there was little room for the rice to expand, the texture is very firm, yet because of the long simmering, it is soft and the fat part of the pork is almost melted. The leaves give a very refreshing aroma to the Tzong. Serve it hot. If it is not salty, use soy sauce as a dip.

I am very sure that many Chinese housewives will protest the method I described. They would rather try to wrap the Tzong in leaves and cook them directly in water. My reason is very simple. I have seen professional wrappers who could manage the wrapping neatly and this is the principal requirement for preparation of this food. When well done, the juice and taste of pork will not lose too much flavor as it is surrounded by tightly packed rice. If not tightly packed, all the taste will go into the cooking water! And the Tzong will never be firm enough. To serve this kind of Tzong, I would rather suggest using the cooking water and making it into a soup.

The Midnight Moon of August

In the thousands of years of Chinese history, the daring Mongolians once succeeded in invading and briefly conquering China. This was the Yuen Dynasty.

Mongolians are very strongly built. During my boyhood, at our National Sport Meetings, no others could match the Mongolians in their game of Mongolian Wrestling. They wore heavy robes with tough hide to guide their legs. They began by holding each other's arms. No one could escape from such a strong grip. Then, with a simple sweep of the leg, the weaker opponent was felled. Mongolians were also well known for their use of the David's Sling to hunt small animals—their accuracy and speed were amazing! Other

Chinese boys used the David's Sling only for distance matches. Mongolians were also excellent horsemen and their horses were noted for their endurance.

They had a great page in history of their invasions all the way to Europe. However, mere strength could not last forever, for without culture, a nation will certainly fail. No one can rule a country without gaining the hearts of the people. So the Yuen Dynasty could not survive.

The Chinese called these invaders the Tartars. Because of continuing unbearable abuse from the ruling Tartars, revolution was secretly sprouting. After their conquest Tartars became more relaxed. They lived among the Chinese and obliged them to fulfill all their daily needs. There were far fewer Tartars than Chinese; however, they were the conquerors and they wanted to live their way.

So a simple plot was planned. All the Chinese people would attack the Tartars at the same time. The planners first started a rumor through a wise man who watched the stars. The star-watcher said a plague would reach the people as a punishment from the gods. In order to divert the plague, the people would have to eat specially made cakes at midnight during the Moon Festival. Soon the rumor was spread throughout the area and every family had a Moon Cake ready to be eaten at the indicated time. The planners were very certain their plot would succeed as the Tartars did not read Chinese.

There were many curious persons, including some Tartars, who couldn't resist trying the cakes ahead of time. All they found was an ordinary cake with slips of paper inside on which were written some characters that looked like a charm. The Tartars could not understand what they meant and the Chinese would never tell. Each little slip of paper actually bore a message: "As soon as you read this slip, go and attack Tartars by any and all means. Everyone of us will do so at the same time—at midnight of the full moon of August." After many battles at various locations, the Tartars lost the war and the Ming Dynasty was eventually born.

TEA

Good tea is a masterpiece of art which can't be copied. The best tea grows only under very special conditions. The tea is planted in the high mountains and is watered only by the natural fog. It grows in such rocky cliffs only the monkeys that have been trained by monks can harvest it. This tea is called Yuen-wu. It is produced in the famous Monte Loo, Kiang-si Province. Literally its name means "Cloudy Fog."

Pre-rain tea is tea harvested before the rain comes. The rainy season comes when the tea is matured. Young and tender tea (pre-matured) is very delicate and expensive. "Double-smoked" tea is tea that has gone twice through the smoking process. The smoking process gives tea a stronger flavor and the double-processing causes the tea to cost more.

The English are famous for their tea which they serve with sugar and lemon, or sugar and milk. Tibetians serve tea with animal lard. It must be very delicious—to Tibetians!

In the Fu-chin Province tea is rated as a high luxury. No metal or porcelain pot is used and only good fountain water, which is heated by a fire made from natural firewood, is used to make the tea. When I was young, I could hardly believe it when they told me that a good teapot can preserve brewed tea overnight even in hot weather. Now I understand it is because a good teapot is made of earthenware which breathes and keeps the tea cool. This is the very same principle of carrying water in a sheepskin bota. I noticed an ad where a man had modernized the bota by lining it with plastic! The advertisement bragged on this feature which completely defeated the purpose for using sheepskin.

I have gathered my knowledge from studying the science of cooking and from experienced friends. The water should be boiled several minutes. This will help to evaporate any added chemical taste. Then the water should cool a little while. This makes a lot of difference as too high a temperature of the water will bring out the bitter taste in tea. Of course water that is too cool is not acceptable either. The brewing time varies. Some good tea takes almost ten minutes. Since the strength of tea is very personal I serve tea to my friends in the following way. I make a pot of very strong tea and serve this with a thermos bottle of hot water for each person to dilute the tea to his own taste. It is surprising but on a hot day a cup of hot tea really quenches thirst. Sipping a cup of good tea is just great on almost any occassion. Tea after a meal helps digestion.

FESTIVAL DINNER

Moon Cake is naturally the most fitting recipe for this tale of The Full Moon of August. But I am wondering if the reader will ever like to try an extremely complicated and time delaying cake making which actually is only used by commercial bakers. Chinese have many festivals during a year. Like other nations too, special dinner parties are given for members of the family to have a chance to be together. Here are some sample dishes using recipes which have been included in this book.

RELIABLE RECIPES

The plan of this book is to link tales with recipes in detail. Now I am selecting recipes with simple but reliable results for readers to practice. Contrary to the first concept of this book, these recipes are in simple words to save the space so that a larger number of recipes may be included. However, the important part of each dish is still explained with remarks. These little remarks turn a recipe into a reliable one but unfortunately many people carelessly skip.

FUNG TZUNG _____

This is a very reliable dish to try, and it has many possible variations depending on the meat used. I use the name of this dish in the Chinese way, which is the classical form in abbreviation, hence it is supposed to be understood what kind of seasoning and cooking method are used.

FUNG — means powder or flour, and in this case it is understood that only rice flour is used. In fact, it is only roughly broken rice, which you can easily prepare with a blender.

TZUNG — means steaming is the cooking method of this dish. It hints to you that no oil is used in this dish but its natural meat fat, and of course it will be a hot to touch dish when it is served.

_____ , this blank, is to be filled with the chosen meat, which can be Pork, Beef, Mutton or Chicken.

However, the procedure is just the same, but the timing will be adjusted to the texture of the meat chosen. In translation into English with a complete name, it should be something like:

STEAMED _____ WITH BROKEN-RICE AND FIVE-FRAGRANT-SPICE

This dish is very popular in many parts of China, except in Cantonese cooking.

To prepare the rice: Use any type utensil to brown the unwashed rice for several minutes. No oil, and only a slight color is required. In fact, this procedure is as toasting the coffee beans, to add a mild aroma which is caused by browning. Then use a blender to break the rice but don't over do it, as we need broken-rice, not flour. You can prepare a good quantity and keep it for later use, say 2 cups of rice.

Spices:

If you cannot obtain the blended Chinese Five-fragrant-spice, I suggest that you blend:

> 1 t. of pepper powder
> 1 t. of cinnamon powder
> 1 t. of ground cloves
> 1 t. of nutmeg powder
> 1 t. of thyme

The original called for spices of Star-aniseed and Flower-pepper corn are not obtainable in most parts of the world. Well, when you don't have a dog, you hunt with a cat!

Meat:

Beef and Mutton should be boneless. The steaming system will break the tough texture, therefore, you can buy the cheap cut. Pork can be boneless or the chops from the shoulder. Only the leg or thigh of the chicken should be used. Wings are good too, but don't use the tips. Breast is not only expensive but a waste as in steaming it turns tough in texture.

Marinade:

For each cup of broken-rice, which will be about enough for each pound of trimmed meat, use:

> 2 T. of soy sauce
> 1 1/2 t. of salt
> 1 t. of sugar
> 2 T. of dry white wine
> 1 T. of water
> 1 t. of the mixed spices.

Marinate the cut meat in the above marinade for at least 30 minutes.

Arranging:

Pick one piece of meat, roll it with broken-rice, set it in a bowl. Arrange neatly in lines at least for the first layer to fill the whole bottom of bowl. Do so until you finish them all. You must still have some more marinade left. In this case, add some broken-rice in the left over marinade to a paste form. Fill the surface of the layer of meat. Cover them and press them flatly and evenly.

Remark:

The right size of bowl is very essential, as it will help you to unmold the steamed meat into another platter for serving. If the bowl is too large, you can unmold it, but the batch will not retain a nicely looking half hemisphere. If the bowl is too small, during the steaming, the rice will swell and it might come out from the bowl. The simple guide is to have a bowl with enough space for the whole batch of meat and broken-rice, yet with another inch to reach the rim. Then when the steaming is done, it will just be full, and you can easily unmold it which in Chinese cooking term, we called it Un-button, while the first arrangement into the bowl was realted to Button the meat in a bowl.

Time in steaming:

The heat should be constantly in boiling point but not necessarily with highest heat. Chicken will take about 30 minutes. The other meats will need more than an hour. Check the doneness with picks.

Remark:

During the steaming, additional water into the steamer might be required to maintain enough steam for the cooking period. Check at least 15 minutes before serving to see if the rice has enough moisture. If not, just sprinkle some water on top. If a proper steamer is not available, use an electric cooker with the dial set at 220 degrees. Remember that most cookers cannot take a bowl too high for its limited space between the bottom and cover of cooker.

DEEP-FRIED BEAN CURD DELIGHT

This is a very good creation and it is worthy for the process which is rather complicate, but very simple.

    2 cups of mashed bean curd
    1/2 cup of minced fish meat, or shrimps
    1 egg
    1/4 cup of broth

Blend the above with the following seasoning:

    1 T. of salt
    1 t. of soy sauce
    1 pinch of pepper and sugar

Place the blended batch in an oiled dish or small baking pan. Smooth the surface with a flat spoon evenly. Steamed at low heat till the batch is firm. Cold it completely, bring it out, cut into domino size. Roll them with the mixture of one part of flour and one part of cornstarch. Deep-fry in oil at 350 degrees till the crust is lightly golden brown.

Since this dish can hardly to determine its saltiness after the additional of flour and starch for deep-frying. You need some sauce as a dipping to serve. Any kind of sauce can be used, say, soy sauce which is most handy one.

The following photo is only one of hundreds vegetarian dishes which consist various kinds of vegetables.

For such kind of dish, the method is normally pre-cooked and a Chinese-frying method of cooking is followed.

Deep fried Squab, see page 44.

Poached Chicken, see page 17.

STEAMED FISH

There are too many different cooking methods for fish. In general, the simplest and best way is to steam it. This section is not written in recipe form, but rather as general information. By understanding these basic rules, you can apply it to many different kind of fish.

The steaming system keeps the cooking area clean, less spattering of oil, no burning fishy smell in the kitchen and much less time to have the fish done. Besides for a fish fancier, a steamed fish holds its natural deliciousness to its utmost.

1. Only very fresh fish should be used for steaming. If your fish is not so fresh, it should be used for some other kind of cooking method, such as deep-frying, etc.
2. Clean the fish, wipe it dry with paper towels, inside and out.
3. If you don't know how to handle a pair of chop-sticks, don't use fish with too many tiny bones.
4. The size of fish should be reasonably medium in thickness. A ten inch sole, sand dab or cod are all right. Salmon should be in slices of no more than an inch thick.
5. When a large fish is to be used, and you like to keep it whole, then you should make several 1/2 inch deep slits on the sides of the fish. Do so at an angle of 45 degrees which will help retain the shape of the fish after it has been steamed.
6. Never add any salt to the fish before steaming as this will draw the natural juice out from the fish. Seasoning can be adjusted after the fish is done.
7. Oil the fish before you place it in a dish for steaming. Always cut some stalks of vegetables handy to form a rack under the fish. This will help the steam go underneath the fish. The preferences are: white parts of green onion, celery, carrot. Don't use others which have too strong a flavor, such as green pepper, or too much moisture, such as cucumber.
8. Always place the fish in the steamer when the water is boiling, and you should keep it boiling constantly.
9. The average time for a medium size fish will be about 12 to 15 minutes. Of course, it varies and you should check it before serving.
10. During the steaming, some condiment and garnishing might be used. In general, chopped fresh ginger root or green onions in strips. Soy bean

paste can be applied on top of fish, especially for Salmon. Fermentated Black beans mashed with garlic is another good combination.

11. For gourmet cooking, the little amount of condensed liquid in the dish on which the fish was steamed, is not to be used. Unless a thickened sauce will be applied, then this liquid should be strained. Add with more broth and seasoning to make a sauce by thickening with cornstarch, and pour on top of the fish before serving. Otherwise, discard this liquid. Sprinkle with salt, garnishing with soy sauce, add more fresh uncooked green onion strips, and burn it with heated oil. The oil should be heated up to 350 degrees in a small utensil, and carefully pour the heated oil on top all over the fish.

12. Fresh Coriander, don't call it Chinese Parsley, it really very good stuff for steamed fish. Since it is not easily obtainable in too many places, omit it and never try to use ordinary parsley.

13. Don't compare with others cooking methods. One of you will not agree with the mentioned rules and argue up to no where. This book is written in English but follows the Chinese cooking *improved* method.

14. Wondering why did the last line have a word of *improved?* Here is a suggestion for those who don't have a proper steamer. Use a pair of roasting pans. It might have enough size to cover two burners of your cooking range at the same time. Fill the lower pan with only an inch of water. Keep the heat high till it comes to a boil, while you leave the other pan, (of the same-size, of course) in the oven to keep it hot, say at 250 degrees. You need a rack like the cookie rack in the boiling water pan, or a saucer to keep the dish with fish, or fishes, for steaming from touching the boiling water. After you place the fish in the boiling pan, on the rack, you place the heated pan which you left in the oven. Why? A cold pan will collect condensation from steaming, which will result in a very poor quality with excessive liquid. Now you start to time. You need about 12 to 13 minutes, and the heat may be kept at medium instead in the beginning which was on high. The only thing you must pay attention, since you don't have a proper steamer, and I don't believe a family size steamer is capable to handle the steaming job better than this improvised steamer with an inexpensive pair of roasting pans, especially if you have to steam six 10 inch fish at the same time, is, you must be careful when the time comes for you to remove the upper pan, which was actually used as a lid. Use a pair of hot mitt, remove the upper pan an inch away, then swiftly pull it aside and turn its upper side down, to

avoid the drippings getting into the steamed fish. I think I have told you quite a lot about how to steam a fish, now I wish you a successful first trying. Be careful not to burn yourself when you remove the upper pan. Do it swiftly and confidently. (Because you don't have a proper handle for you to hold, on such a roasting pan used as a lid).

I cannot deny that modern technology put Chinese old time designed tools obsolete, but I still think that Chinese knew what they wanted—a bamboo steamer is definitely scientifically designed.

The photo below is a Drunken Fish dish cooked by Chinese-frying method. Because the fish had been marinated, you only need very little adjusting of seasoning in this dish.

   8 oz. of marinade fish fillet
   1 t. of chopped ginger roots
   some finely cut ginger strips and carrots for garnishing
   3 T. of oil
   1 t. of sesame oil

Heat the oil, put in the rest, cook for 2 minutes. During the cooking, some more cooking wine should be used to create enough steam to help the cooking done in shorter time, which retains the firmness of fish.

STEAMED BEAN CURD

    1 cup of mashed bean curd
    1 egg roughly beaten
    1 t. of salt
    1 t. of soy sauce
    1 pinch of pepper and sugar
    1 stalk of chopped green onion
    1 T. of oil

    Mix the above thoroughly and fill a shallow oiled dish. Steam at medium heat for about 12 minutes till it is firm. Add in 1 t. of soy sauce on top, blend it with the top layer juice to form a pleasing color before serving.

THE ILLUSTRATOR

In every field of endeavor, excellence may be sought; and it can be achieved with the ingredients of good taste, understanding and love. With these thoughts in mind, this book was conceived, planned, and written.

Many Chinese of my age and background could easily recount these traditional tales. My only inspiration was to link the tales with recipes and to have charming illustrations for each tale. But to find such an artist is like seeking a white peacock! It is difficult for most Chinese brush painters to adapt to the perspective required for book illustration, and those who are able to do so often lack knowledge of Chinese traditions and literature. Vainly I searched . . .

Playing golf countless times, I never that had done;
Hitting the ball just like this, I have a hole-in-one.

When living in South America, I was very impressed by an illustrator whose drawings frequently appeared in a famous Chinese weekly magazine, now known as "Today's World." Chinese histories, appearing in synopsis form, were beautifully illustrated under the artist's pen name of "White Feather." In each issue of this same magazine there was a short romantic story in modern style, illustrated with appropriate drawings by an artist called Polly Ko. The styles of the drawings in the two sections were entirely different. I imagined that "White Feather" must be an elderly Chinese for these were traditional brush strokes; I assumed Polly Ko to be a young girl, because her soft pencil tones conveyed tenderness.

Still in search of my "white peacock," I visited Hong Kong recently. My friends there knew of my search and gave me many suggestions. I politely refused a recommendation of the merits of Polly Ko and mentioned that I hoped to meet "White Feather." Imagine my surprise when I was informed that "White Feather" and Polly Ko were one and the same. A rare white peacock indeed!

Polly Ko is a charming person and an excellent artist. She has the gift of insight so necessary for visual interpretation of these tales. Humility is essential in Chinese manner, but I hope to be forgiven if I say that with her artful drawings, this book cannot fail to be unique.

If you, reader, enjoy the book, share my feelings, and understand that woven into this book are many lonely hours of research and contemplation, then I can unhesitatingly end this page with a famous Chinese expression: What A Pleasure!

INDEX

One of the prominent differences between men and other animals is that we human beings can communicate through writing; and writing can be conveyed to a distance without losing its meaning.

To end this book, there is nothing left but to wish you, reader, joy in reading it. Then the famous Chinese phrase may be repeated again: "What a pleasure!"